BUDGET TRAVEL IN JAPAN

Penny Farrant

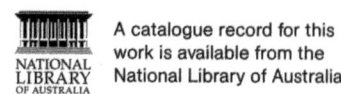 A catalogue record for this work is available from the National Library of Australia

BUDGET TRAVEL IN JAPAN
by Penny Farrant

© 2021, PENNY FARRANT, PERTH, AUSTRALIA

All rights reserved. No part of this book may be reproduced, stored in a retrieval system, or transmitted in any form or by any means, electronic, mechanical, recording or otherwise, without the prior written permission of the author and copyright holder.

The information, views, opinions and visuals expressed in this publication are the sole expression and opinion of its author.

TEXT: Penny Farrant.

PHOTOGRAPHS: Penny Farrant; Cover photo: Bill Farrant.

ISBN: 978-0-6485088-0-9 (paperback)

PUBLISHER: Penny Farrant; for special orders email: pennyfarrant@gmail.com

BISAC CODES: Travel, Asia East, Japan TRV003050

COVER PHOTO: Tulips at Hitachi Seaside Park (Photo: Bill Farrant).

ACKNOWLEDGMENTS: Special thanks to Diana Iles, Annette Bradford, Judith Harris and Bill Farrant for proof-reading and providing invaluable feedback & Helen Iles (Linellin Press WA) for publishing advice.

Contents

	INTRODUCTION: Skiing, Sightseeing visas & Seniors — *Japan: December 1991–January 1992*	5
1	Shinkansens, Sushi & Shrines — *Fukuoka: 1-19 September*	9
2	Ohashi, Open-top bus & Okonomiyaki — *Fukuoka: 20-29 September*	13
3	Izakaya, Ikebana & Iceberg lettuce — *Fukuoka: 30 September-14 October*	17
4	Dazaifu, Disaster centre & Dinners — *Fukuoka: 15-29 October*	21
5	Whale sharks, Water droppers & White heron — *Osaka & Himeji: 30 October-3 November 2016*	25
6	Stone paths, Shinto shrines & Sweet fish — *Kumano-Kodo: 4-11 November*	29
7	Mikan mochi, Manatees & Maglev — *Ise & Nagoya: 12-16 November*	33
8	Shikoku, Sculptures & Sashimi — *Takamatsu, Naoshima & Kurashiki: 17-23 November*	37
9	Christmas lights, Cars & Ceramics — *Hiroshima, Fukuoka & Saga: 24 November-3 December*	41
10	Mitsubishi, Minamiaso & Murataya ryokan — *Nagasaki, Takamori & Kumamoto: 4-13 December*	45
11	Puppies, Pottery & Plates — *Okinawa: 14-20 December*	49
12	Tofuyo, Tunnels & Tug-o'-war — *Okinawa: 21-31 December*	53
13	Calligraphy, Capes & Caves — *Okinawa: 1-12 January*	57
14	Snorkelling, Star-sand & Sugar — *Yaeyama Islands & Naha: 13-20 January*	61
15	Mud, Mochi & Monkeys — *Fukuoka & Beppu: 21-28 January*	65
16	Super ring, Sand dollars & Subtropical plants — *Aso & Aoshima: 29 January-2 February*	69
17	Ferry, Farmed shrimp & Flying fish — *Yakushima: 4-11 February*	73
18	Animatronics, Active volcanoes & Akune — *Kagoshima, Izumi & Okayama: 3 & 12-19 February*	77
19	Mitsu, Miso fish & Morning market — *Matsuyama & Uchiko: 20-25 February*	81
20	Chicken necks, Camellias & Chinkabashi — *Sukumo, Shimanto & Cape Ashizuri: 26-28 February*	85
21	Yuji, Yakatabune & Yuzu — *Kochi & Niyodo: 1-5 March*	89
22	Pilgrims, Pacific & Pools — *Cape Muroto & Tokushima: 4 & 6-11 March*	93
23	Snow, Sightseeing train & Sand spit — *Iya Valley & Miyazu: 8 & 12-15 March*	97
24	Tori, Tulips & Temples — *Kyoto: 16-23 March*	101
25	Gardens, Golden temple & Geisha — *Kyoto: 24-30 March*	105
26	Seismic isolation, Stepping stones & Sculptures — *Nara & Kobe: 22 & 27 March*	109
27	Bear bells, Bananas & Blowfish — *Nakasendo Way: 31 March-9 April*	113
28	Azaleas, Animal cafes & Antiques — *Tokyo: 10-20 April*	115
29	Parades, Pandas & Parasitology — *Tokyo: 21-30 April*	121
30	Whiskey, Wedding couple & Wisteria — *Yokohama, Hitachi & Ashikaga: 23 & 27 April*	125
31	Romance, Ropeway & Rhododendrons — *Hakone: 1-7 May*	129
32	Birds, Bonsai & Brakes — *Saitama & Tokyo: 8-15 May*	133
33	Ceremony, Crafts & Crackers — *Saitama & Tokyo: 16-23 May*	137
34	Historic district, Hida & Hoba miso — *Takayama: 24-30 May*	141
35	Soba, Snow wall & Skunk cabbages — *Nagano: 31 May-3 June*	145
36	Kites, Kamo aquarium & Kitchen equipment — *Niigata & Tsuruoka: 4-11 June*	149
37	Tsuguharu, Turning dolls & Tanbo art — *Akita, Hirosaki & Kuroishi: 12-15 June*	153
38	Bicycles, Best film & Big bath — *Tazawako & Yamagata: 16-23 June*	157
39	Samurai, Soymilk skin & Shiki-shima — *Nikko & Tokyo: 24-28 June*	161
40	Picking cherries, Polar bears & Poppies — *Sapporo, Asahikawa & Daisetsuzan: 29 June-3 July*	165
41	Black-haired beef, Boats & Boardwalk — *Wakkanai & Rebun Island: 4-10 July*	169
42	Sea angels, Sumo & Shells — *Monbetsu & Abashiri: 11-16 July*	173
43	Brown bears, Binoculars & Buoys — *Rausu & Shiretoko: 17-20 July*	177
44	Marimo, Mining & MOO — *Teshikaga & Kushiro: 21-26 July*	181
45	Farms, Foxes & Fog — *Otofuke & Shinhidaka: 27-31 July*	185
46	TV tower, Tonden & Tozai line — *Sapporo: 1-8 August*	189
47	Tokyu hands, Temiya line & Takino — *Sapporo & Otaru: 9-19 August*	193
48	Snow festival, Ski jump & Stonehenge — *Sapporo: 20-28 August*	197
	Practical tips & advice	202
	INDEX	204

ABOUT THE AUTHOR:

Dr Penny (Penelope) Farrant was born in Melbourne, Victoria but lived most of her life in Sydney, New South Wales, where she retired in 2015 before moving to Perth, Western Australia, in 2019. She has degrees in architecture and marine biology and is particularly interested in the art-science interface. She is the author of *Colour in Nature — a Visual and Scientific Exploration* (Blandford UK 1997) and *Pen-Pen's Journey* (Vivid Publishing Fremantle WA 2016). Her interests include art and calligraphy, swimming, bushwalking and travel.

Penny and her husband Bill have visited Japan three times. Their first visit was for five weeks in 1991–1992, at which time they fell in love with the country and made a plan to return for an entire year after they retired. They took up the challenge and spent a year in Japan in 2016–2017. As seniors on a limited budget, they travelled the length and breadth of Japan for a whole year, during which time they met many of the locals, learnt a lot about Japanese culture, sampled a range of interesting and delicious foods, and enjoyed a wealth of remarkable and exciting experiences. They returned to Japan for three months in 2018 and intend to visit again.

Penny's accompanying book *Gluten-Free Travel in Japan* is rich with food photos and describes how Bill, having been diagnosed with coeliac disease in his 50s, faced the additional challenge of having to avoid foods containing wheat, barley, rye and oats. Penny sent a weekly email to friends during their year away, with photos and descriptions of their experiences, and those emails form the basis of both books.

Skiing, Sightseeing visas & Seniors
Japan: December 1991–January 1992

Above: Restaurant, Kushiro; Below: Wearing Ainu costumes at restaurant, Kushiro, 1992

INTRODUCTION: Japan December 1991–January 1992

Skiing

We travelled to Japan for five weeks in 1991–1992 to visit friends and see some of the country. We spent a wonderful week with our friends in Sapporo, where we did all the things you can do in the heart of a Japanese winter, such as skiing at the local and olympic ski runs, swimming at the big indoor pool complex, eating out, watching the snow festival displays being constructed, and shopping in the underground malls. We then travelled around the four main Japanese islands using Japan Rail Passes — sadly having to miss those places in Hokkaido that weren't accessible due to snow. We fell in love with Japan and made a retirement plan to spend a year exploring the country and seeing it in all seasons.

After we retired in 2015 we decided to act on our plan. We blocked out our calendars for a year but did little more than that until my brother phoned one day to ask if we wanted to join him and his friends on the Kumano-Kodo Pilgrimage walk in the Japanese autumn. Jolted into action, we decided to do the Kumano-Kodo walk with his group, and decided to also book for the Nakasendo Way walk in the following spring.

We organised our year around the two walks, as well as the weather — so as to be down south in winter and avoid the snow, and up north in summer to avoid the heat. And after deciding to spend a couple of months at language school in Fukuoka (cheaper than Tokyo!), it seemed sensible to do this at the start of the trip during the autumn typhoons.

Sightseeing visas

With a plan in hand, we did the paperwork and applied for special six-month sightseeing visas (to be extended by six months in Japan), as well as sending off our 'yakkan shoumei' (medicine importation) forms. Planning the trip was challenging — we had to arrange for a friend to mind our house, we had to pay our bills in advance, and we had to fix or arrange a hundred other things at home — besides making bookings and arrangements for our time in Japan, all of which would be on a seniors' budget!

Seniors

But it was truly worth it. We wholeheartedly recommend Japan as a destination for senior travellers, or anyone with a limited budget. It has everything you could want: it's safe; it's clean; it's relatively cheap; it's quiet (no speaking on the phone on public transport); the people are friendly, polite and honest; seniors are respected; it's easy to get around; it's interesting and exciting; there's no tipping; the facilities are amazing; the technology is incredible; everything works — including the multitude of really handy vending machines; convenience stores are excellent and everywhere; cars are driven on the left hand side; the food is fantastic, cheap and delicious; there's good accommodation to suit every budget; the health care system is excellent, efficient and cheap; the public transport system is logical and efficient; the trains run on time — so you can make bookings with very short transfer times and be fairly confident that you can make the connections; the cities are interesting and exciting; there are beautiful landscapes in the countryside and national parks; and, best of all, the toilets are not only clean, but amazing — everywhere you go.

The classification and the benefits of being a 'senior' in Japan are a bit hit-and-miss. The age for a senior is usually regarded as 70, however it is sometimes 65 (look for '65' or '70' in the signs at entrances to museums and gardens, and wave your passport at the ticket window because foreign visitors often get discounts!). In other places, such as local swimming pools, seniors' benefits only apply to residents living in the immediate local government area.

We lived our dream of returning to Japan and spent a whole year, from September 2016 to August 2017, exploring the country further and seeing it in all seasons. This is a record of our year in Japan, based on the weekly emails we sent to friends and family back home in Australia and elsewhere. Needless to say, we've been back to Japan again since, and we hope to keep returning. We are now hooked on sumo and avidly watch the six Grand Sumo Tournaments each year.

Photo Page 5: Ryusei no taki, Sounkyo Gorge, Hokkaido, 1992

Above: Sounkyo Gorge; Below Left: Mount Fuji; Below Right: Train to Shikoku, 1992

Below: Outdoor onsen, Tazawako, 1992

Shinkansens, Sushi & Shrines
Fukuoka: 1–19 September

CHAPTER ONE

Above: Leopalace21 apartment, Kasuga; Below: Studying in apartment   Above: Cooking class, Furukawa Cooking School, Ohashi

FUKUOKA: 1–19 September

Welcome to Japan!

Our welcome to Japan in 2016 was a fabulous view of Mount Fuji, entirely cloud-free, glimpsed from the plane as we flew from Sydney via Tokyo to our new 'home city' of Fukuoka in western Japan.

We started our year in Japan by spending the first two months at a language school in Fukuoka. Our accommodation had been arranged by the school and was a tiny apartment with a small kitchen/laundry/bathroom area, a separate toilet, lounge/bedroom/dining room with wardrobe, and loft with a ladder (about a metre of headspace so we used it for storage).

We immediately loved Fukuoka as it was very laid back and uncrowded with nice people and not too much traffic — a lovely place to spend a couple of months. Fukuoka is about the same size as Sydney and, although we were living in one of the suburbs, it was easy to get around and into the city by means of good train, subway and bus systems.

Shinkansens

As well, the high-speed shinkansen trains go from Fukuoka's Hakata Station to many other parts of Japan. They are frequent, comfortable and convenient — and so fast that you can actually travel the length of Japan in a single (long) day. However, they are also expensive if you don't have a Japan Rail Pass. With our special six-month visas, we weren't eligible to buy JR Passes. They are only available if you have a temporary three-month visa, in which case they can be used on all but the express Nozomi and Mizuho shinkansens. But, be aware that there's only a small space dedicated for large luggage, so you need to travel light and get on at the right end of the carriage!

Shinkansens are not only fast, but also safe — all the shinkansen lines are inspected daily after they knock off at midnight — and they are cleaned frequently. One day we watched the cleaners line up on the platform and all enter and exit the train in sync. They looked very businesslike in matching uniforms and cleaning gear, and all bowed as one after they alighted from the train, before marching off in line.

Photo Page 9: Hakozakigu Shrine, Fukuoka

Sushi

Kyushu is the fruit and vegetable centre of Japan and both are plentiful and cheap. In fact food in Japan is mostly cheap, and a good meal can cost around $10–$15. We were lucky to have a Yayoiken set meal restaurant and a Hamazushi sushi restaurant very close to our apartment.

Each Wednesday our school organised a cultural activity, the first of which was Hakata doll (ningyo) painting followed by a sushi lunch — fun and relaxing, and a good break from classes. On Saturday one of our teachers organised a 3½ hour cooking class at the Furukawa Cooking School, after which we visited the Nanzoin Temple to see the largest reclining Buddha in the world, located outside the city centre in a beautiful rural area. On the way home we enjoyed a delicious Indian meal in Hakata, the upmarket side of the city across the river.

Shrines

Our next cultural activity was a visit to the week-long Hojoya Festival, held each September around the Hakozakigu Shrine. Hojoya is a Shinto festival for acknowledging living things that we eat or otherwise use in our daily lives. While the shrine itself is at the centre of the event and everyone visits it and the various surrounding exhibitions, there are also stage performances and other types of entertainment over the week of the festival, and a very large area of the festival space is devoted to food stalls and sideshows (shooting galleries, fish/eel/crab/toy shark catching, horror shows). Streets and streets of them. It was relatively uncrowded when we arrived in mid-afternoon, but by evening it was shoulder-to-shoulder. It was all very colourful and the foods very interesting and beautifully presented. More and more people were wearing yukatas (summer traditional clothes) as the night wore on, and the incoming trains were packed.

Shinto is Japan's traditional religion, with most Japanese seeming to practise the rituals, often in addition to Buddhist practices. Frequently shrines and temples of the two religions can be found adjacent or intermingled at the one site.

Above: Hamazushi sushi restaurant, Kasuga; Below: Reclining Buddha, Nanzoin

Above: Monk with begging bowl, Hojoya Festival

Ohashi, Open-top bus & Okonomiyaki
Fukuoka: 20–29 September

Above: Teachers & students, NILS Ohashi language school; Below Left: Bus stop near apartment, Kasuga; Below Right: Local fruit and vegetable shop near Ijiri Station

FUKUOKA: 20–29 September

Ohashi

We were enrolled at the Ohashi campus of the NILS Language School in Fukuoka. Ohashi is on the train line to the Tenjin area of central Fukuoka. At the time, the courses were tailored for people wanting to do 1, 2 or 3-month short courses and you could join in at any time starting on a Monday. The classes were small — three students in mine and three in Bill's (the other students were from US, Malaysia, Scotland and Singapore). It was full on for four hours each morning, four days a week. After class we would all go out for lunch to wind down, before going home to study. Our classes seemed relentless, with never enough time in the day to put into study, although Bill and I usually managed a swim on the way home, at one of the two local swimming pools — just to keep up a bit of physical fitness while our brains seem to be becoming more and more frazzled.

The classes were pretty much all in Japanese, with very little English spoken or written. Even though they were quite challenging, there was always room for a bit of fun. One day the head teacher tried vegemite for the first time (and loved it!). You could buy vegemite and other foreign foods at Kaldi Coffee Farm, a shop in the city. And the cultural activities on Wednesdays were always fun and relaxing, and a good break from classes.

Students came and went. A new student from Tennessee joined our group during the week and we farewelled a Malaysian classmate at a French restaurant near to our accommodation after her final presentation at the school. When students left they had to give a short presentation in Japanese to all staff and students before receiving their graduation certificate.

Open-top bus

The fourth week's Wednesday cultural activity saw the class divided in two. Most went to a ramen-making session, while we (no-red-meat and gluten-free) were sent on the open-top bus tour of the city. Had we known that the others were actually making noodles, not just eating them (alas, they were full of wheat and in a pork broth) we would have opted to make noodles but not eat them. Our alternative was very dismal, sitting on the top (and only) floor of an open-top bus on the seaside tour of the city on a wet day. The rain was torrential and we got a thorough soaking. The ponchos provided weren't up to the job and there was no way we could get a camera out to take photos. The only lighter moments were when the commentary suggested admiring the views and taking memorable photos. We could barely make out the landmarks, and what we could see of the ocean certainly wasn't blue. It no doubt would have been lovely on a fine day! After the bus tour our teacher took us to a bookshop, where we were amazed at the system in place — go to a console, type in the name of the book, press 'print' if a picture of the book comes up on the display, take the printout to a counter a metre away, where the shop assistant phones the relevant floor, and the book is waiting for you at the counter on that floor when you arrive to pick it up.

Okonomiyaki

One Saturday we were lucky to chance upon a community event at the local historical museum, where two domes house historical burial urns from the Yayoi period (300 BC to 300 AD). We sat on the grass watching and listening to taiko drums, flute performances and a variety of children's craft activities.

That night we cooked our own version of okonomiyaki — a savoury pancake made from seasoned flour, cabbage and other vegetables, and/or meat and decorated with a special sauce, mayonnaise, bonito flakes, and sometimes an egg.

One week there were only two days of school lessons because of two public holidays (one was Respect for the Aged Day) and our Wednesday activity. Despite a typhoon warning being issued that week (if a typhoon hits Fukuoka, everything closes down), we only received heavy rain and strong winds. Afterwards the temperatures were in the 30s and although the sun came out several times, it was mostly behind high clouds or interspersed with rain deluges, so the humidity was very uncomfortable.

Photo Page 13: Yayoi funeral urns, Kasuga

Above: Taiko drums at community event, Kasuga

Above: Dome housing Yayoi burial urns; Below: Class whiteboard, Ohashi

Above: Yayoi burial urns inside dome

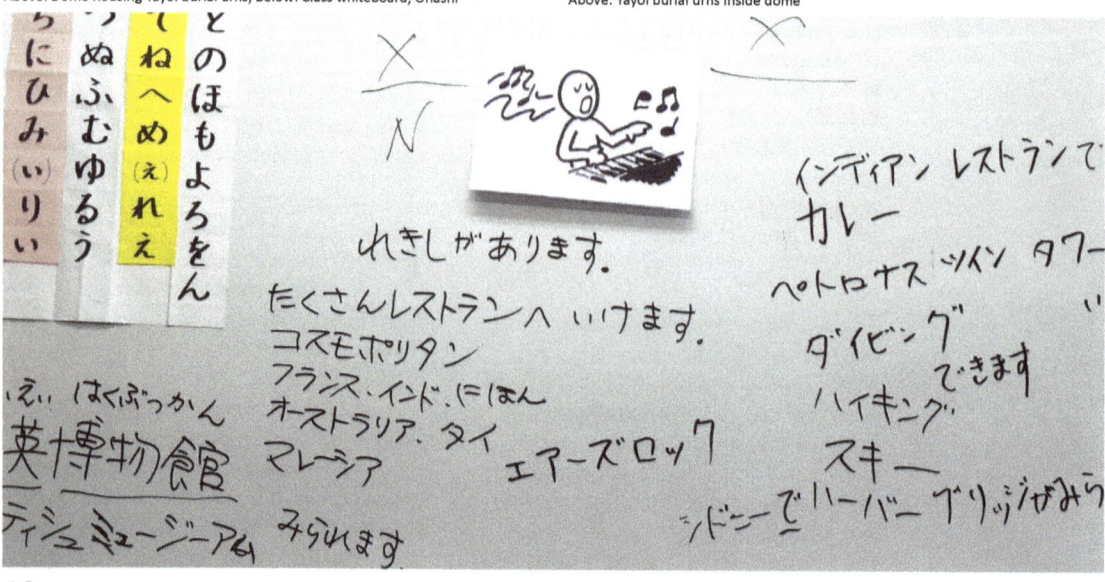

CHAPTER THREE

Izakaya, Ikebana & Iceberg lettuce
Fukuoka: 30 September–14 October

Above: Fruit display, Iwataya Department Store; Row Below: Izakaya party

FUKUOKA: 30 September–14 October

Izakaya

Our next class cultural activity was an izakaya party — basically an eating and drinking after-work party. Ours was held at Yaburekabure, one of the local restaurants, where our headmaster had booked a private room. All students and teachers attended. The room held two long low tables and we sat on cushions on tatami mats, fortunately with our legs accommodated in a sunken area below the tables — which was good for people with long legs like Bill! The two tables separated the smokers from the non-smokers. Yes, smoking was allowed!

Drinks were ordered — ranging from beer and shochu (a distilled drink about midway in alcohol content between wine and spirits) to soft drinks and iced tea. Each person ordered a dish from the menu, and these and other extra dishes were shared amongst everyone at the table. The food was plentiful and delicious and included sashimi, sushi, omelette, salads, tempura, pickles and yakitori. As more beer and shochu were consumed, tongues loosened and the conversations became lively and interesting. Our teachers encouraged us to practise our Japanese, which was fun.

Ikebana

The following Wednesday our cultural activity was ikebana, Japanese flowering arrangement. The appreciation of flowers in all seasons has played an important role in both Shinto and Buddhist religions for centuries and ikebana, regarded in Japan as one of the esteemed classical arts of refinement, is extremely popular.

Both of us did particularly well, with the teacher mentioning Bill's 'perfect' stem lengths and my 'perfect' posy-making abilities. She even suggested I should have a flower-arranging licence! This was despite the fact that she removed every stem from both our arrangements (and everyone else's) and completely re-organised them. We think her praise wasn't so much due to our skills, but rather because we were the only ones in the class who had watched the recommended You Tube video prior to attending the lesson.

One of our teachers kindly gave us tickets to an ikebana display in the top floor of the Iwataya Department Store, which we attended one afternoon. The display of 149 works attracted mostly well-to-do middle-aged women, as befitting the venue. Afterwards we went down to the basement food hall of the department store where you could buy a single musk melon for around $150. The same women were spending up big down there! Yet, strangely enough, about ten metres away there were fruit and veggies in our price bracket. The displays were amazing. At the checkout they added a small ice-pack to each refrigerated item and wrapped every bottle in bubble-wrap.

Iceberg lettuce

Another school cultural activity was a visit to a fake foods sample workshop. The majority of restaurants in Japan advertise the meals available using a display of very realistic reproductions in the shop window, so you can choose what you want to eat before you go in. The Fake Food Workshop Riki is a two-man operation in a small building in Fukuoka. The workshop display was incredible. There were even fake octopuses and squids on top of the toilet cistern! We were each given a little basket and a calculator and a budget of 1620 yen (about $20) to spend on decorations for making our own parfait or cookie cake. Between us, Bill and I made one of each. We applied hand-made decorations to a base of fake sauce and fake cream, which we piped into our plastic parfait glass or cookie (flan) base. Each would have cost around $40. The highlight, though, was seeing how fake tempura and fake iceberg lettuce were made. It was truly incredible and easy, using wax and bowls of water of different temperatures. The workshop was also set up with various props that made for great fun photo opportunities.

At the weekend we ventured out to Yanagawa (about an hour away) for a four-kilometre punt trip along the canals and a visit to the Tachibana museum. This museum houses a collection of art and crafts from the Tachibana family, which controlled the Yanagawa clan throughout the Edo period.

Photo Page 17: Restaurant, Kasugabaru

Above: Yayoi hundred yen community buses; Below: Canal, Yanagawa   Above: Fake Food Workshop Riki

CHAPTER FOUR

Dazaifu, Disaster centre & Dinners
Fukuoka: 15–29 October

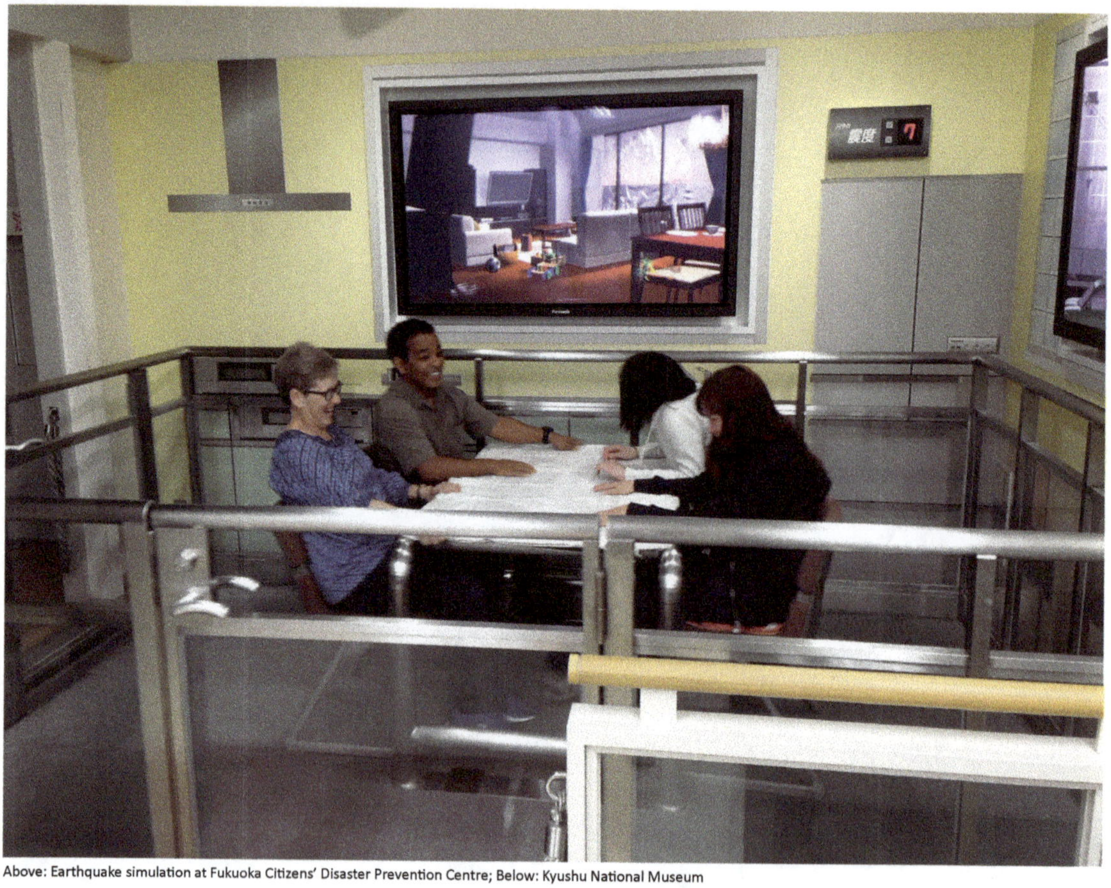

Above: Earthquake simulation at Fukuoka Citizens' Disaster Prevention Centre; Below: Kyushu National Museum

FUKUOKA: 15–29 October

Dazaifu

One Saturday we took a ferry to Shikanoshima, an island just off Fukuoka, where we bicycled right around the island, had our first swim in the sea, and enjoyed an amazing lunch at one of the local restaurants. The following day a group of us went to a visiting exhibition of ancient scrolls depicting frolicking animals. It was a beautiful exhibition, though we had to queue for a total of three hours to get to the actual exhibits! It was at the Kyushu National Museum, a spectacular modern building set into the hillside at Dazaifu, site of the government 1300 years ago and site of the ancient Tenmangu Shrine. The Dazaifu area is extensive, with many shrines, gardens, souvenir and food shops — and tourists.

There are otherwise very few tourists in Fukuoka compared to other cities in Japan. The local people are very quiet, unhurried and well mannered. Phones have to be on silent on all forms of transport and talking on the phone is frowned upon, as is eating on the street. When sitting down next to someone on the bus, it is customary to make a small bow. No-one ever crosses a road unless the light is green. The traffic lights take ages to change but everyone is prepared to wait, and when turning corners, buses and cars stop at pedestrian crossings — just on the offchance a bicycle or pedestrian might come along.

Disaster centre

Our class cultural activity days in our final two weeks of language school took us to Yusentei Park, a beautiful traditional Japanese garden built in 1754, where we had matcha tea and sweets in a tatami room overlooking the lake, and to the Fukuoka Citizens' Disaster Prevention Centre located near Fukuoka Tower and Fukuoka Dome (the latter is a venue for baseball and concerts). At the Disaster Centre we experienced, by way of simulations, a 7-magnitude earthquake, a 100 km/hr typhoon, opening a car door in a flood, opening the door of a building against rising floodwaters, and escaping a burning building through smoke. We also had hands-on experience extinguishing flames using a fire extinguisher. There was a wardrobe of outfits, as well as a fire truck, for photo opportunities.

One day after class we visited an onsen (hot spring) in a rural area about half an hour away and spent a lovely hour or so relaxing in the various hot and cold, indoor and outdoor pools and saunas (men and women were in separate areas) and afterwards enjoyed a lovely barbecue meal at a restaurant within walking distance of our apartment.

On one weekend, one of our teachers drove us to Itoshima Beach, about an hour and a half away from Fukuoka, to see a shrine in the ocean with 'lovers' islands' tied together behind it. We had an Hawaiian-style lunch at a beachside restaurant, then visited Fukuoka Tower, which featured Halloween decorations as well as the obligatory lovers' props. Like the rest of the buildings in Fukuoka, the Tower is height-restricted because the airport is located within the city. Another afternoon we took the train to Kurume to see a display of flowering cosmos, which was very pretty even in the rain.

Dinners

On 29 October we finished our two months at school, wishing we were more proficient at speaking the language. We had a farewell at the school and were presented with certificates by the headmaster along with cards signed by all the other teachers, after giving our five-minute speeches — in Japanese of course! Bill impressed them with photos of Sydney and I showed photos and spoke about our pet birds.

After our graduation we had lunch with the rest of our classmates, dinner with one of the teachers at an amazing seafood restaurant in the city, and lunch the next day with three other teachers who lived near to our apartment and who had been helping us with various 'outside of school' problems such as obtaining a storage locker and getting the wi-fi working in our apartment. They were all lovely, kind people and it was sad to leave them and to leave Fukuoka — even though we knew we would be returning to the storage locker several times during the next five months to swap things around.

Photo Page 21: Barbecue restaurant, Kasuga

Above: Bicycling around Shikanoshima

Above: Storage locker, Kasuga

Above & Below: Graduation day, NILS

CHAPTER FIVE

Whale sharks, Water droppers & White heron
Osaka & Himeji: 30 October–3 November

Above: Osaka buildings; Below: Halloween toy whale sharks, Osaka Aquarium   Above: Museum of Oriental Ceramics, Osaka

OSAKA & HIMEJI: 30 October–3 November 2016

Whale sharks

Osaka is famous for having one of the largest aquariums in the world — big enough to house whale sharks — so we were looking forward to our visit there. Predictably, the shinkansen trip from Fukuoka to Osaka was fast and enjoyable.

When we arrived at Osaka's Umeda Station, we had to negotiate our way to an Airbnb supposedly five minutes away. We couldn't even find the location of the first of 30 'how-to-get-there' photos, but eventually managed to find the place 45 minutes later using our phone apps (maps.me and Google Maps) — once they started working after we got out of the underground 'web'. We found out later that the route was through Japan's biggest underground shopping mall, where every intersection had around five choices of direction, in addition to the mall having a number of different levels.

The Osaka Aquarium Kaiyukan, with a fabulous whale shark display and tunnel tank, didn't disappoint. It specialises in displaying marine life from right around the Pacific Rim, with 15 huge tanks each re-creating a specific region. There was a central tank containing two whale sharks and a huge variety of other fish. Some of the memorable animals on display were rockhopper penguins, sunfish, giant deepwater spider crabs, and a giant isopod. Being Halloween, members of staff were dressed according to the theme and there were also appropriate displays of toy animals and other objects decorating the aquaria.

Water droppers

It was a bit colder in Osaka than in Fukuoka and the leaves were starting to change colour, especially near the river in the beautifully peaceful cultural precinct in central Osaka where we visited the Museum of Oriental Ceramics. Here we saw an exhibition called 'Charm of the Scholar's Desk — Water Droppers of the Joseon Dynasty', which featured 126 exquisite examples of water droppers. These delicate, beautiful, small pieces of ceramics were used to pour water into inkstones and were important items that decorated scholars' desks alongside their brush, ink and paper.

A visit to Osaka Castle (a full scale replica of the original) and surrounding parklands was a must. The original Osaka Castle was built in 1583, and in 1997 the latest of many restoration projects was completed — with the intent of restoring the main tower to its Edo-era splendor following a multitude of other restorations over the years. The castle is a concrete reproduction of the original, and the interior operates as a modern, functioning museum that includes elevators.

We also enjoyed a trip to the Nanko Wild Bird Sanctuary. The Nanko Wild Bird Sanctuary, in an outer part of Osaka, is a reclaimed area full of water birds and serious bird-watchers. There are many walkways, waterways, and an excellent observatory where visitors can relax out of the weather and observe birds out in the marshlands through viewing windows.

White heron

Another day we took a fast train out of Osaka to visit Himeji Castle and its adjoining Koko-en garden, both of which rate highly amongst the must-see places to visit in Japan, for good reason. Himeji Castle dates back to the 14th century and is listed as a UNESCO World Heritage Cultural Heritage site, as representative of Japanese wooden castle architecture.

The 'White Heron' main keep of the castle has white plastered walls and is so named because it resembles a white heron in flight. The castle's original shape and beauty have been kept through many restorations, but unlike other castles in Japan, it hasn't ever been rebuilt or moved, and it retains the internal stairways and rooms throughout its six storeys (plus basement).

The exquisite Koko-en garden adjacent to Himeji Castle was constructed in 1992, using techniques from the Edo period (1600–1860). Located on the former site of the feudal lord's west residence, it covers 3.5 hectares and consists of nine walled gardens designed in various Edo period styles — including a tea garden, a pine garden, a bamboo garden, a flower garden, and the garden of the lord's residence with a pond and waterfall.

Above: Himeji Castle Nishi-Oyashiki-Ato (Koen-en) Garden; Below: Himeji Castle

CHAPTER SIX

Stone paths, Shinto shrines & Sweet fish
Kumano-Kodo: 4–11 November

29

Above: Onsens in valley, Yunomine Onsen; Below: Autumn colours, Koyasan   Above: Nachi Taisha Shrine

KUMANO-KODO: 4–11 November

Stone paths

The Kumano-Kodo is one of only two UNESCO World Heritage Pilgrimage walks (the other is the Camino in Spain) and our walk took us to some of the most significant and sacred locations in Japan. They are the locations where Buddhism was first adopted. We spent nine days walking on the ancient stone paths of the Kumano-Kodo pilgrimage trail. On most days of the pilgrimage walk the trail went through small villages, along some sections of road, and sometimes our route involved train, bus, taxi and minibus transfers. But most of the walk was through forest, along mossy stone paths that were often quite slippery and often very steep.

The biggest day was day seven, which included the section from Koguchi to Nachi Taisha Shrine, with an 800-metre climb over four kilometres up said slippery paths, and then down said slippery paths. The total ascent was 1200 metres over a distance of 15 kilometres. Everyone managed to do it, although knees and backs were sorely tested.

Shinto shrines

Along the way we passed hundreds of small shrines and religious sites and visited the two very important shrines at Hongu and Shingu, as well as the outer and inner shrines at Ise, where the most important Shinto shrine in Japan is located and which every Japanese believer must visit at least once in their lifetime.

Accommodation on the walk ranged from a Buddhist monastery at Koyasan, to luxurious Japanese inns (ryokans), a converted school, and a modern hotel. All had onsens where we could relax our weary muscles before enjoying delicious meals. All lodgings had beer, plum wine and sake available for further relaxation of weary walkers.

On day one we met up with our walking group of nine plus guide (a Japanese-speaking French-Canadian from Nagoya, who was excellent), at the Il Cuore Hotel in Namba, Osaka. This was an evening 'meet-and greet' session at an izakaya restaurant near the hotel. Day two saw us on a train from Osaka, although we only got as far as Hashimoto due to a landslide on the rail line. We joined the huge crowds waiting for buses, but eventually managed to get a few taxis to get us closer to our destination, then caught a bus into Koyasan. We then walked the 7.5 km women's pilgrimage route around the perimeter of Koyasan, which had wonderful views. Koyasan itself was full of glorious autumn foliage.

The walk took us to the Oku-no-in Cemetery, in Koyasan, a huge place that kept us busy until nightfall, after which we made our way to our shukubo pilgrim monastery lodgings. The lodgings were very comfortable, with televisions and kerosene heaters in each room (though it became a bit chilly in the night after we had turned the heater off). All meals at the monastery were vegetarian, plentiful and delicious. It was a special treat to be invited to join the early morning prayers and fire ceremony the following morning.

After breakfast on day three, while still in Koyasan, we visited the head temple of Kongobuji before being transferred to Takajiri-Oji for lunch and to the start of our afternoon walk. We stayed in Takahara, a rural hamlet, that night.

Sweet fish

On Day four we walked to Tsugizajura-Oji from where a vehicle took us to our two-night accommodation at the Ryokan Yunomineso just outside Yunomine Onsen. Here one of our dinners included sweet fish on skewers. On day five we visited the very important Hongu Taisha Shrine, and on day six, after leaving the ryokan, we walked to Koguchi.

After our huge climb on day seven, the final accommodation at Kii Katsura was at the luxurious modern hotel complex of Nakanoshima, on one of the two islands that were used for James Bond films. On day eight, we viewed the aftermath of the morning's tuna auction on our way to the station to catch a train to Shingu. After another train to Ise, home to Japan's most revered shrine, we visited Geku, the outer shrine of the Ise Grand Shrine, then enjoyed a delicious final evening group meal together in Ise before saying our farewells the next morning.

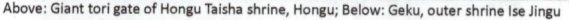

Above: Giant tori gate of Hongu Taisha shrine, Hongu; Below: Geku, outer shrine Ise Jingu

CHAPTER SEVEN

Mikan mochi, Manatees & Maglev
Ise & Nagoya: 12–16 November

Above: Shinkansen display, JR Railway Park, Nagoya; Below: Periodic table display, Nagoya City Science Museum

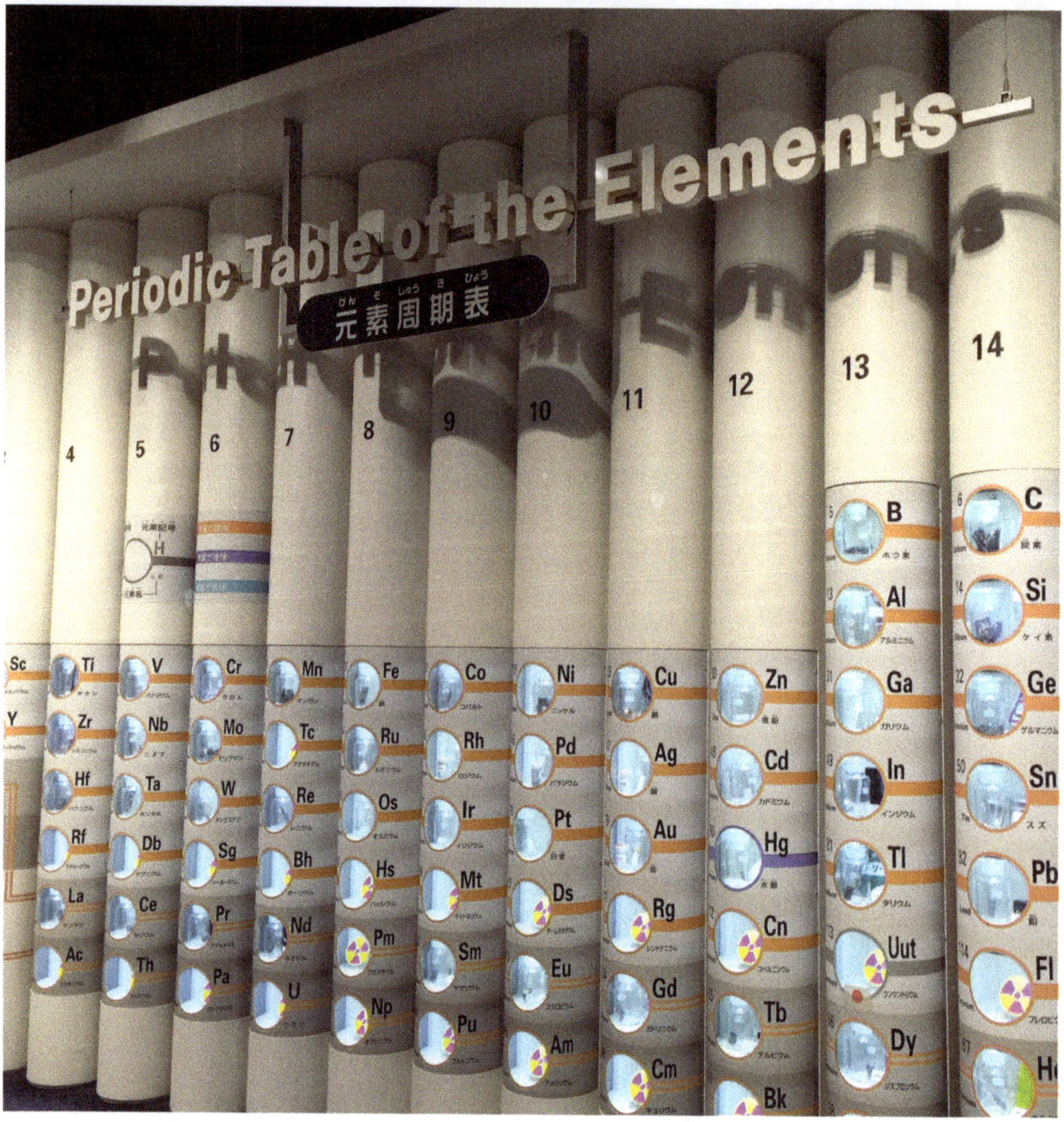

ISE & NAGOYA: 12–16 November

Mikan mochi

The morning after the walk I developed muscle spasms in my right hip, no doubt as a result of the 800 metre ascent and descent on the last day, so, rather than visiting the final shrine with the rest of the group that morning, we moved into our Airbnb — which was, as luck would have it, only a hundred metres from the hotel where we were staying with the walk group on the final night, and very close to the inner Ise Grand Shrine — then took a taxi to the nearest hospital.

The medical staff were very efficient and kind and I was given three types of medicine to take over the following week. Luckily, walking slowly on the flat was ralso recommended as 'good medicine', so the rest of the day was spent in Ise walking the kilometre or so to Naiku or Kotai Jingu, the inner shrine of the Grand Ise Shrine, located about six kilometres from the Toyouke Daijingu, or Geku Outer Shrine that we had visited the previous day.

The Ise Grand Shrine (Ise Jingu) is the most important of all the Shinto sites in Japan and is very large, with 125 shrines. The narrow street running parallel to the main road to Naiku is lined with souvenir shops and restaurants and we listened to a taiko drum performance along the way before finding a small restaurant serving bowls of tiny fish on rice for lunch.

The Airbnb we stayed at was a room within a guest house, and we shared the kitchen and other facilities with the hosts. During our time there we met two of the four hosts, one of whom was a Buddhist monk and the other a rickshaw driver. The place was cosy and it was great to sit and chat over a glass or two of sake, practising our Japanese with one of the hosts while he cooked up some chicken breastbone cartilage for his dinner. We had bought mikan mochi (pounded rice balls with sweet mandarins inside) that we could share with him.

Manatees

On our second day in Ise we took the train intending to go to Kashikojima, where a recent G7 conference had been held. Because the first train we took in the morning terminated at Toba, we decided to visit the Toba Aquarium 'before the crowds' but ended up spending most of the day there as it claimed the most species of any in Japan and was easily the best one we'd been to.

There was a sea lion show, an entertaining walrus show and a 'penguin walking' show featuring Humboldt penguins. There were also manatees, dugongs, finless porpoises, Commerson's dolphins, amazing displays of invertebrates in tanks, including a fascinating display of live nautiluses of varying sizes and a nautilus hatchery. There were no whale sharks or whales but Toba Aquarium had real quality displays, including all sorts of marine animals from the local Ise Bay and many of the smaller animals, such as invertebrates, that aren't normally represented.

We did get to Kashikojima later in the day, though everything had all but closed down by then. So we only managed to get in a short walk around the harbour and past the entrance to Shima Marineland.

Maglev

From Ise we travelled to Nagoya where we had the tiniest Airbnb apartment imaginable, but with real beds. We visited the Nagoya City Science Museum where we saw fabulous exhibitions of electrical discharge and tornados, watched the planetarium show, and experienced the -30°C deep freeze lab with photos of the aurora australis taken from the Japanese base in Antarctica.

We also visited the JR Railway Museum in Nagoya, an interesting and relatively new place with everything you'd want to know about shinkansens and the new 500+ kilometres/hour Maglev that will come into commission in 2027. Unfortunately we missed out in the ballot for driving the shinkansen simulator! The Rail Museum featured a huge diorama of model train lines, with a half hour show with live commentary replicating a (much speeded-up) 24-hour night-day cycle. Like many cities in Japan, the Nagoya parks and streets featured beautiful nighttime illuminations.

Photo Page 33: Our Airbnb host was cooking chicken cartilage for his dinner

Above: Nagoya park illuminations; Below: Walrus show, Toba Aquarium

Below Left: Nautilus hatchery, Toba Aquarium; Below Right: Commerson's dolphins, Toba Aquarium

CHAPTER EIGHT

Shikoku, Sculptures & Sashimi
Takamatsu, Naoshima & Kurashiki: 17–23 November

37

Above: Ritsurin Garden, Takamatsu

Above: Canal, Bikan Historical Area, Kurashiki; Row Below: Okayama Koraku-en

TAKAMATSU, NAOSHIMA & KURASHIKI: 17–23 November

Shikoku

Our next stop was in Takamatsu on Shikoku Island, staying in a spacious Airbnb decorated by a very trendy interior designer. The place was close to Ritsurin Garden, where we spent a few hours roaming around lakes and viewing its beautiful features. Later on we made a return visit for the opening of the garden's nighttime illumination season.

On one day we took a day trip on the ferry from Takamatsu to Teshima, one of the 'Art Islands' to visit the incredible museum there, designed by artist Rei Naito and architect Ryue Nishizawa. Unfortunately no photos were allowed inside! The museum is a single concrete flying saucer-shaped building, in fact a single room, built into a hillside, with two large rounded openings to the sky. Inside, visitors wearing plastic foot coverings are mesmerised by the path of water droplets coming up through holes in the floor. This may sound weird, but the impact was nothing short of amazing. We walked the six or so kilometres back to the port, enjoying the stunning views over the sea and multitude of islands. The road went mostly through forest, though there were small villages, individual houses, small industries and farms dotted along the way.

Sculptures

The Art Islands comprise a group of islands that feature modern art and architecture, originally set up in an attempt to stimulate the declining economy but which have now become vibrant and world famous. Once every three years there is a huge art festival, the Triennale, in which artworks expand onto other islands and mainland ports.

We left Takamatsu the next day and took a different ferry over to the Art Island of Naoshima, famous for its Yayoi Kusama pumpkin sculptures, where we spent two nights at the luxurious Benesse House, full of modern art that you otherwise wouldn't get to see. The hotel also has its own Museum of Art as well as sculptures scattered in the grounds. Nearby are the Lee Ufan and Chichu Museums, the latter containing among other delights, a room with five Monet paintings displayed to such perfection that they take your breath away. The meals at Benesse House were exquisite, individually designed to suit our dietary requirements and with our own individually printed menus.

From Naoshima we travelled to Kurashiki on the main island of Honshu and while there we took a train trip to spend a day at the Koraku-en Garden in Okayama, one of the three finest gardens in Japan. Here, like Ritsurin, the autumn colours were magnificent and many families were dressed in traditional clothes and having their photos taken by professional photographers using a variety of props, such as parasols.

Sashimi

After two nights of luxury on Naoshima, we didn't have high expectations for the Youth Hostel in Kurashiki, especially as it was out of town on the top of a very steep hill full of gravestones (which we found out later was the biggest burial mound in Japan). When we arrived at Kurashiki Station we left our heavy bags at the car hire depot next door to the station, from where they were picked up by the Youth Hostel host sometime during the day and delivered to our accommodation. Thus we were not only saved from having to take the luggage on a bus and up a very steep hill, but we could go straight away to investigate Kurashiki's beautifully restored old section of town and canal.

The Youth Hostel seemed like a long way from anywhere, but turned out to be excellent. We had our own private room that was very comfortable. We shared the place with a girls' cycling team on the first night but, as the only guests there on the second night, we were the only ones enjoying a six-piece band rehearsal in the lounge room. The host recommended a terrific seafood restaurant at the bottom of the hill for dinner on our first night and on the second night we found a yakitori (chicken skewers) restaurant, which was both good and interesting. We tasted a little of the chicken sashimi but declined the chicken intestines, livers and necks. The Youth Hostel host and his wife put together gluten-free breakfasts for us that were substantial, delicious and cheap (around $8 each).

Photo Page 37: Lee Ufan Museum, Naoshima

Above: Teshima Art Museum Visitor Centre & Restaurant

Above: Sculpture, Benesse House; Below: Benesse House Museum

Above: Yayoi Kusama Pumpkin, Naoshima

CHAPTER NINE

Christmas lights, Cars & Ceramics
Hiroshima, Fukuoka & Saga: 24 November–3 December

Above: Atomic Bomb Dome at night, Hiroshima; Below Left: Miyajima 'floating' shrine; Below Right: Brewery chimney, Saijo Sake Town

Below: Figurines, shrine on Mount Misen

HIROSHIMA, FUKUOKA & SAGA: 24 November–3 December

Christmas lights

We had a lovely time in Hiroshima, where we spent five nights at a K's House Hostel. There are several of these hostels around Japan and they're great because they are cheap, clean, friendly and well located (and have won awards). We had a tiny room with a large double bed and a small ensuite. However, there was a roomy common area, washing facilities and an excellent kitchen, as well as a rooftop garden that would be even more pleasant in warmer weather.

The essential places to visit in Hiroshima are, of course, the Atomic Bomb Dome, the Peace Park and its multitude of memorials, and the Peace Memorial Museum, all of which were still as moving as we remembered from our visit in 1992. Although part of the Museum was being refurbished, the main building was still full of interesting displays.

On a later night we walked to the illuminations along Peace Parade in the city, the main themes being Christmas and Peace. It was pure bling. Everything that didn't move had lights on it. Away from Peace Parade, however, the Atomic Bomb Dome, lit up internally at night, was quite otherworldly.

We decided not to re-visit Hiroshima Castle but were keen this time not to miss the World Heritage listed Itsukushima Shrine and 'floating' tori at Miyajima, which we visited early one morning to escape the crowds and to catch the high tide. After viewing the shrine and floating tori we went to the top of Mount Misen on the ropeway and walked the extra 150 metre climb to the summit. When we returned to the bottom, there were huge crowds at the shrine below.

Another day trip we did from Hiroshima was by express bus to Sandankyo Gorge, supposed to be the most beautiful ravine in Japan (we would agree that it is particularly beautiful). We walked for a couple of hours. Then a ferryman took us across the gorge to a small restaurant where we ate sweet fish and chicken on skewers cooked over hot coals, before returning to the entrance where there was a conveniently located onsen for a hot spa before the 1½ hour bus trip back to town.

Photo Page 41: Old brewery, Saijo Sake Town

Cars

We had to make a booking for the English-speaking tour of the Mazda Museum and factory, and the tour turned out to be so fascinating that 1½ hours wasn't nearly long enough. The Mazda site is roughly seven kilometres across in both directions and takes up a good part of Hiroshima city and port. There are two assembly lines, each around a kilometre long, which rely on a mix of human workers and robots. Interestingly, they mix up the models on the assembly line, with three different models being built on one line at the same time. One car is completed every 15 hours.

After the Mazda factory we spent the afternoon at Saijo, home to seven different sake breweries, where we even tried some sake icecream. Lunch was at the excellent Hana-temari restaurant, which boasted two local wheat-free specialty dishes: deep-fried chicken and lotus coated in rice flour (komekara), and a hot-pot of chicken and vegetables cooked in sake (bishunabe).

From Hiroshima we caught a shinkansen back 'home' to Fukuoka where there were gorgeous blue and silver illuminations. We stayed at the really convenient Sunlife Hotel right by Hakata Station, with very small rooms but great breakfasts.

Ceramics

After swapping our luggage around (in our outdoor rented storage unit) we departed on a two-week trip around the north of Kyushu. Our accommodation at the Saga Youth Hostel was amazing — a huge room with twin beds, table and chairs, balcony and TV, plus our own fully accessible toilet (huge, with all the mod cons) and separate shower/bath room. It was certainly roomier and grander than anywhere else we had stayed. Saga is famous as a venue for hot-air ballooning, so we visited the balloon museum and did a simulated flight with Bill at the controls. It's also close to the famous ceramic centres of Arita, Imari and Karatsu, and we spent all day Saturday at Arita (museums, clay mine and 1000-year-old gingko tree being the highlights). Saga too was alight with illuminations and light shows.

Above: Sandankyo ferry; Below: Museum Arita, Kyushu Ceramic Museum

Above: Saga Balloon Museum

Above: Roadster, Mazda Museum

CHAPTER TEN

Mitsubishi, Minamiaso & Murataya ryokan
Nagasaki, Takamori & Kumamoto: 4–13 December

Above: Peace statue, Peace Park, Nagasaki

Above: Grassy replica of Mount Fuji, Suizenji Jojuen, Kumamoto; Below: Earthquake damage, Kumamoto Castle

NAGASAKI, TAKAMORI & KUMAMOTO: 4–13 December

Mitsubishi

A highlight of our visit to Nagasaki was a visit to Hashima (also known as Gunkanjima or Battleship Island), where some of the scenes from the 2012 James Bond movie 'Skyfall' were filmed. Bookings had to be made over a month in advance. Being weather dependent, there was still no guarantee that the trip would go ahead or that a landing would be possible. So we were extremely fortunate to go and to be able to land! The island functioned as a Mitsubishi coal mine until 1974, and held (and still holds) the record for the highest population density in the world. Back in Nagasaki, the Gunkanjima Digital Museum was nothing short of amazing.

There was plenty to do for five days in the beautiful city of Nagasaki. The atomic bomb ground zero (hypocentre) and Peace Museum were very moving, and the Glover Garden very interesting. We also had dinner one night at the top of the ropeway where there was a 360-degree view of the city.

We visited the Nagaski Penguin Aquarium, which has 180 penguins of nine species (including temperate and sub-Antarctic penguins), and where the penguins have their own harbour beach. On display was a beautiful poster called 'Christmas present', showing the king penguins out on the lawn when it snowed one Christmas day in Nagasaki.

Minamiaso

From Nagasaki we travelled via Kumamoto to Takamori, a small town on the southern outer rim of the Mount Aso caldera. Mount Aso is the largest active volcano on earth and is constantly billowing smoke and ash. Fortunately we had been to the top and looked inside it in 1992, as the ropeway was now closed due to the April 2016 earthquakes. We had to get a bus to Takamori because one of the rail bridges had been destroyed and there was a lot of earthquake damage to roads and buildings in and between Takamori and Kumamoto.

A single carriage train, painted with anime cartoon characters, was operating along a 10-minute section of the railway track on the Takamori side of the collapsed bridge. We took the train one day and walked further on to two other stations, one boasting the longest station name in Japan (Minamiaso Mizuno-Umareru-Sato Hakusui-Kogen Station) and the other boasting the only onsen located in a train station — though unfortunately closed due to earthquake damage. On another day we took a similar route along the valley visiting most of the 12 beautiful natural springs using electric-assisted bicycles hired at the station.

Murataya ryokan

In Takamori we stayed at the Youth Hostel Murataya Ryokan, a former ryokan or Japanese inn. We had our own tatami room with a bay window looking towards the volcano and a sunny verandah with two chairs overlooking the street. The sake brewery was on the next corner and there were several restaurants, a supermarket and shops where we could buy meals. We had excellent Japanese breakfasts at the Youth Hostel and the lady of the house prepared our family-sized private bath each night at about 5.30. About a kilometre out of town was a 'Tunnel Park' that boasted a half kilometre-long abandoned tunnel chock-a-block with Christmas trees and lights, all hanging above a gushing flow of spring water. At the blocked end of the tunnel was a display of modern light and sound art.

After we left the Mount Aso area we spent several days in Kumamoto. Close to the Youthpia Youth Hostel where we were staying was Suizenji Jojuen, a beautiful 'tsukiyama' garden, containing grassy replicas of important mountains such as Mount Fuji, as well as various shrines. Unfortunately the two main attractions in Kumamoto — the Castle and the Zoo/Botanical Gardens — were both closed because of severe damage suffered during the earthquakes, though we were able to walk around the perimeters. There was also an excellent cultural museum with plenty of interactive displays about the Castle. Kumamon bears (the mascot of Kumamoto) were everywhere, as was evidence of earthquake damage (including at the Youth Hostel).

Photo Page 45: Gunkanjima (Battleship Island), off Nagasaki

Above: Mount Aso, from Takamori

Above: Ganbare Kumamoto! Manga Yosegaki Train, Takamori; Below Left: Tunnel Park, Takamori;: Below Right: One of 12 geosite springs in the Aso area

CHAPTER ELEVEN

Puppies, Pottery & Plates
Okinawa: 14–20 December

Above: Noborigama hill climbing communal kiln, Yomitan, Okinawa

Above: Ryukyu Glass Village; Below: Toy puppies for sale, main street Naha, Okinawa

Above: Decorating lacquerware

OKINAWA: 14–20 December

Puppies

We flew to Okinawa for the Christmas-New Year period to stay in Itoman, a fishing port about a half hour south of the capital Naha.

We had an Airbnb apartment there for a month, which was quite roomy by Japanese standards, and had everything we needed. The apartment was one floor up above a barber's shop and a builder's office. This suited us fine because the ground level was only 2.2 metres above sea level according to the tsunami warning sign on the lamppost outside. We had a very good supermarket nearby, and the Fish Centre, Growers' Market and Itoman City Market were about 25 minutes' walk. Both the supermarket and Growers' Market had a small range of gluten-free food items. Our local beach was about ten minutes' walk away from the apartment, but initially it was too windy and chilly to venture into the water and it seemed that no-one swam there in winter anyway, even though the box jellyfish nets had been removed!

The city of Naha is very touristy and Americanised because of the military bases north of the city, with steaks, taco rice, beer, loud music, loud colours, Hawaiian shirts, and interesting souvenirs (puppies, thongs, cane-toad purses and rubber chickens).

Pottery

Fortunately Bill had found out, on a search of the internet, that the Yomitan Pottery Village, about two hours north by bus in the middle of the main island, was having its annual festival on a weekend soon after we arrived. Thousands of gorgeous pieces of pottery are sold at reduced prices at this festival and it is very popular. Indeed, people were buying a lot of pottery!

The village was established about 40 years ago by four now-famous Japanese potters, and consists of about 20 different pottery 'houses' and one glass-blowing 'house'. The houses have their own kilns, but are centred around a huge communal 'noborigama' or multi-chambered climbing kiln (it climbs up the hill) which they fire up several times a year.

Photo Page 49: Noborigama hill climbing communal kiln, Yomitan, Okinawa

We met potter Kinjo Meiko, whose American helper was able to explain everything to us. Hot roasted purple sweet potatoes were the go for lunch.

One day we took a bus about five kilometres south from Itoman to the Ryukyu Glass Village where they make beautiful hand crafted glass objects of all kinds. ('Ryukyu' is the name of the entire chain of islands stretching from Kyushu to Taiwan). There we made our own drinking glasses by blowing molten glass into a mould and rolling it to create the final shape of the top. We had to collect the glasses a few days later, so we enrolled in a nearby lacquerware class for the day we had to return.

Plates

While searching on the internet we had come across this beautiful little-advertised lacquerware shop offering classes, and it turned out to be just down the road from the glass factory. We each decorated a lacquerware plate using the special local Ryukyuan technique of 'tsuikin', in which lacquer (gum from the lacquer tree) is mixed with pigments to create a putty that is cut, carved and coloured before applying. We were instructed not to use the plates for a few months while the putty lost its toxicity and set properly, so we posted them home to Australia by surface mail.

Ignoring the sign warning about cone shells, blue-ringed octopuses, sea snakes, striped catfish, scorpion fish, stonefish and long-spined sea urchins, we went for a swim at our local beach one day. There were plenty of tropical fish to see in the warm, clear water.

We visited the famous Churaumi Aquarium and Ocean Park on a weekday. It was two hours by express bus, but well worth it to see the huge whale sharks and the show featuring dolphins and false killer whales. Where else in the world could you sing along to 'Santa Claus is Coming to Town' while swaying your arms side to side and having Santa conduct two whales and four dolphins standing upright with their heads and shoulders out of the water as they swayed and sang with the crowd? Interestingly, false killer whales have very loud voices!

Above: Whale shark, Churaumi Aquarium and Ocean Park

Above: Dolphin & false killer whale show, Churaumi; Below: Beach at Itoman

Above: Palms in Arboretum, Churaumi

CHAPTER TWELVE

Tofuyo, Tunnels & Tug-o'-war
Okinawa: 21–31 December

53

Row Above: Itoman Peaceful Illuminations

Above: Cornerstone of Peace, Peace Memorial Park, Itoman; Below: Commanding Officer's Room, Former Navy Headquarters, Naha, Okinawa

OKINAWA: 21–31 December

Tofuyo

Christmas Day morning was our quietest morning in Japan so far. We were told that everyone would be sleeping off the previous night's partying. And yes, we found it was true that Kentucky Fried Chicken is the choice of food for lunch/dinner at Christmas — and that it must be ordered well in advance.

On Christmas evening we went to the local Itoman Peaceful Illuminations with our Airbnb hosts. It was very crowded with people and traffic. The lights were spectacular and included a large botanical glasshouse with lights throughout, as well as light tunnels, illuminated fake palm trees and flowers, a stage with music, and wine tasting.

The venue was Itoman Farm, a winery/restaurant that once boasted zebras and other exotic animals roaming around the grounds. There were huge queues for all the photo opportunity setups, the children's illuminated train, the stretch limo with interior illuminations, and for the food stalls. On the way home we visited the Peace Memorial Park, three kilometres away, where the car park was being used for shuttle buses to the illuminations. The Memorial Park was also the location of another illumination, the Pillar of Peace, which consisted of five beams of laser light stretching four kilometres vertically into the air. It was quite spectacular.

Boxing Day was just a normal working/school day, so we walked over to do a tour of the Masahiro Brewery nearby, to learn a bit about awamori. Awamori is a distilled liquor about the same strength as whiskey, made from high quality Thai rice and black koji (a fungus). It is a specialty of Okinawa and is delicious.

Later on we sampled 'tofuyo', a three-year-old fermented tofu soaked in awamori, somewhat between caramel and blue cheese in taste and texture. It's eaten in tiny quantities while drinking alcohol and is really exquisite. On the way back from the brewery we visited Bibi Beach, a summer tourist venue with gorgeous beaches, but closed for swimming in winter because of the 'cold' 23°C water.

Tunnels

We spent one cool, windy and rainy morning in Naha at the Manko Wetlands Centre, where there's a boardwalk through the mangroves and mud flats. Amongst other birds we spotted two of the rare black-faced spoonbills (only 2000 in the world). The centre itself is an educational facility, free to enter, and well equipped with good quality binoculars and identification charts for bird viewing.

From there we walked to the fascinating former Japanese Navy Underground Headquarters, where we saw the commanding officer's room, operations room and tunnels dug with hoes and picks, and learnt about the Battle of Okinawa as well as about the demise of a quarter of the Okinawan civilian population in the Second World War.

Tug-o'-war

Another day we invested in a day-pass on the monorail to see various attractions around the capital, Naha. We visited Shurijo Castle, which was mostly a reconstruction because of damage sustained during the Battle of Okinawa. We also visited the Giant Tug-o'-War Monument — Naha is famous for its annual tug-o'-war, using the largest ropes in the world — then we had lunch in the city at the Makishi Public Market, in the Heiwa-Dori Street market town area. Here you can buy your fish on the first floor and have it cooked on the second floor, though we settled for a set meal of prawns in fermented black bean sauce with rice. The man next to me at our table was drinking zero alcohol beer — popular in Japan with its zero alcohol driving limit and drinking age of 20.

Our local Growers' Market (the largest in Okinawa) sold all the 'healthy' Okinawan food — lots of purple sweet potatoes (beni-imo) and other purple veggies, various coloured carrots, many different greens, seaweeds and other unusual things, as well as a variety of snacks made from sweet potatoes. The local Itoman Fish Centre was also very good, and there was a small tofu factory a few doors up from our apartment where we could buy several types of fresh warm tofu from about 6 am every day except Tuesday.

Photo Page 53: Tunnel, former Japanese Navy Underground Headquarters, Naha, Okinawa

Above: Tsunami sign on lamp-post outside Airbnb   Above: Itoman City Market; Below: Giant tug-o'-war rope, Naha

Calligraphy, Capes & Caves
Okinawa: 1–12 January

Above: Python, Okinawa World; Below: Minatogawa Man and cave cafe, Valley of Gangala

OKINAWA: 1–12 January

Calligraphy

Over New Year the supermarkets were open but most tourist places were closed for several days. We were caught out with the buses, however, on 23 December, not realising it was the Emperor's Birthday public holiday, and consequently had to wait quite a while for a bus.

Our Airbnb hosts kindly invited us to join their family for New Year's Eve. Among others, we met our host's aunt, whose kind offer of a calligraphy lesson I took up a couple of weeks later. New Year's Eve itself wasn't unlike an Australian New Year's Eve, with lots to eat and drink, kids running riot, and men and women in separate clusters watching the concert in Tokyo on TV. However the count-down on TV involved crossing over to bells tolling in each of 108 different places across Japan. After midnight we walked to the local shrine and joined a long queue of people giving short prayers, receiving a drink of awamori and buying fortune papers.

Capes

On the holiday weekend we visited a snorkelling spot about half an hour's bus trip to the south. It was a bit windy and faced the Pacific Ocean, but was protected by the outer reef and there was plenty to see underwater. And no sharks were spotted, despite a warning sign. We had to organise our own snorkelling trips because the commercial snorkelling tours didn't accept anyone over 60! Later in the week we snorkelled at Cape Maeda, supposedly the number one snorkelling spot on mainland Okinawa. Conditions weren't good but there was a small lagoon protected by both the outer reef and a ring of rocky islands. The water was shallow but the underwater fish and coral life were extraordinarily good.

We also snorkelled at Mibaru Beach one day, along from the glass bottomed boats, and another day at Tokashiki Island, which we visited with our Airbnb host. Tokashiki is very hilly, and has lovely views and beautiful calm azure bays with white coral sand. Being the off season, it was very quiet. We didn't see any whales, but the season for whale-watching trips had started here a couple of weeks previously. On another day, despite near gale-force winds and rain, and because we had pre-purchased one-day bus passes, we ventured up north to Cape Manzamo, a wild and woolly headland with spectacular cliffs. We weren't the only ones there, however, as there were busloads of other tourists — mostly Korean and Chinese.

Caves

After New Year we visited Okinawa World, a local theme park with an Okinawan village, Okinawan crafts (hands-on weaving, paper making, indigo dyeing, glass blowing, pottery, screen printing), a tropical fruit orchard, a habu snake show (the habu is the most common deadly snake in Okinawa), a habu awamori brewery (distilled drink with a habu snake in the bottle), and Okinawan dancing with taiko drums and a dancing lion-dog. At the entrance, everyone got to strike the big taiko drum once, to herald the New Year. There were plenty of photo and animal handling opportunities, including hedgehogs, which were the latest pet craze in Japan.

A huge limestone cave system runs underneath Okinawa World, with a one-kilometre walk through (and stalactites cut to accommodate walkers!). The cave walk was particularly impressive, with not too many signs, good non slip surfaces, subtle lighting, and a bank of aquaria near the end displaying cave animals. The only unusual thing was a 'cave mailbox' where you could buy, write and send postcards. Later on we returned to do the nearby Valley of Gangala walk, through a valley formed from a collapsed limestone cave complex. Because the Ryukyu limestone is alkaline, 14,000–20,000 year old fossils of an early hominid known as 'Minatogawa Man' have been preserved here. Judging by the pictures shown by our guide, Minatogawa Man was quite a handsome chap!

We also fitted in a trip to Okinawa's most sacred site, the World Heritage listed Sefa-utaki. Here there are six 'Ibi' or sanctuaries, where rituals and ceremonies were held over a period of 400 years from 1470. For lunch we opted for fruit smoothies rather than the snake stew!

Photo Page 57: Calligraphy lesson, Itoman

Above: Tokashiki Island; Below Left: Shisa, Itoman; Below Right: Local Shinto shrine

Below: Snorkelling, Cape Maeda

CHAPTER FOURTEEN

Snorkelling, Star-sand & Sugar
Yaeyama Islands & Naha: 13–20 January

Above: Kabira Beach, Ishigaki Island; Below Left: Sugar fruit drinks and sugar cane processing; Below Right: Water buffalo cart, Taketomi

Below: 30 July 1978 monument — the day that Okinawa reverted to driving on the left

YAEYAMA ISLANDS & NAHA: 13–20 January

Snorkelling

After Itoman we spent a week in Ishigaki in the Yaeyama Islands, pretty much as far south as you can go in Japan. The weather was cool, windy and rainy for the entire time, but we couldn't complain as most of Japan was getting very heavy snow. We went on a snorkelling boat trip the day after we arrived, despite the tour operator suggesting we might want to cancel because the water temperature was down to 23°C and the air temperature was around 20°C. We did get cold after an hour in the water because of the wind and the ill-fitting wetsuits, and decided to get out sooner rather than later — the man had told us not to overdo it at our age and we didn't want to prove him right! The snorkelling wasn't bad because the water was clear and the fish life was prolific. However 70% of Ishigaki's corals had been affected by the high summer water temperatures (31°C).

The most interesting meal of the week was at a local restaurant in Ishigaki. (Un)fortunately the deep-fried spam and avocado was only on offer for lunch, so we had to settle for soft deep fried tofu, barbecued leeks, potatoes with squid, and a chicken dish.

Star-sand

One day we took a ferry over to Iriomote Island, in the Iriomote Ishigaki National Park and home of the rare Iriomote wild cat (a lynx), of which there are only 100–150 remaining. The usual port was closed, due to the rough seas, so we got a bus halfway around the island to the starting point of the jungle cruise we had planned. The boats go up the Urauchi River for about eight kilometres. Iriomote is mountainous with high rainfall and jungle, lots of ferns, including tree ferns, and the island has the largest stand of mangroves in Japan. There wasn't a single cat to be seen and we were told there was more chance of seeing one at night, when they tend to be hit by cars.

We walked for an hour up and an hour back in pouring rain through the jungle, effectively into the centre of the island, to see the two waterfalls. With three hours to wait for a return bus, we got a lift from the man at the river cruise office to Star-sand Beach — where the sand is made up of protozoan skeletons — after which we walked to the (closed) port to wait for a bus to the port that was operating.

Sugar

Using five-day bus tickets, on another day we visited the north-western beaches of Yonehara and Kabira. The former beach was mostly closed due to rip currents but we were able to snorkel at one end, and this beach had the best snorkelling and the best corals we had seen so far in Japan. Kabira Beach was beautiful and features on all the travel brochures. However swimming isn't allowed because of glass-bottom boat traffic. We also visited a grove of the endemic palm trees (*Satakentia liukiuensis*), after which we bought fruit drinks made with pineapple/guava + sugar cane juice + blocks of cane sugar. The sugar cane was being processed into juice and sugar on the premises. We also took a bus ride to the most northerly point of Ishigaki, to see the Hirakubozaki Lighthouse and magnificent views.

On another day we visited Taketomi Island, only a ten minute trip by fast ferry from Ishigaki. The town on the island has been restored to traditional condition, so all the houses have red tile roofs and stone walls, including the Youth Hostel (where we had considered staying, but had thought it too risky in case we were to get stranded on the island if the ferries were cancelled due to rough seas).

We walked around the town and to two of the beaches, one of which was a designated swimming beach with functioning showers. It was pleasant, although there was little to see underwater and we had to endure a huge number of encroaching cats in the picnic area, possibly attracted to the salmon sushi we'd brought for lunch. The weather was quite hot and there was a warm breeze which was delightful because it carried with it vast numbers of butterflies. The weather turned cold when we returned to Naha (18°C), where we stayed for one night, bought some ceramic shisa (lion-dogs) and went to the beautiful Tsuboya Pottery Museum, which had been closed on our last visit.

Photo Page 61: Kiln at Ikutouin Pottery Studio, Naha

Above: Urauchi River cruise, Iriomote Island; Below: Traditional house, Taketomi

CHAPTER FIFTEEN

Mud, Mochi & Monkeys
Fukuoka & Beppu: 21–28 January

Above: Pounding rice for mochi; Below: Umitamago Aquarium, Oita

FUKUOKA & BEPPU: 21–28 January

Mud

We left Okinawa and flew back 'home' to Kyushu, where we were reunited with the balance of our luggage. We had been using a storage locker up till now, having taken full advantage of the generous Qantas luggage limit, but we couldn't possibly carry all our gear around after leaving Fukuoka for good. All thoughts of hiring a car and camping had gone with winter approaching, so the camping gear had to be sent home.

Car hire would have been too expensive and stressful — not so much the driving as the parking, which is a real problem in Japan unless you are staying in top range hotels, because there is no on-street parking. And as for camping … well, it snowed the day after we arrived back in Fukuoka (same latitude north as Sydney is south) and campgrounds were likely to be closed in winter, like the beaches.

We stayed in Fukuoka to extend our visas, which took several hours, and to deal with the luggage, which took a few days and a lot of paperwork. So, we found out where the Department of Immigration had moved to, and we learned all the ins and outs of mailing parcels via Japan Post and sending suitcases by international courier (easiest if it's only stuff you brought with you).

While in Fukuoka we had dinner at a restaurant called 'Camp Hakata', which featured great vegetable curries. The restaurant was decorated with camping gear — a reminder of the gear we were sending home unused.

We left Fukuoka after a few days and took an express bus to Beppu, a couple of hours away. Beppu has the most onsens of any place in Japan. Our hotel had its own lovely onsen with indoor and outdoor pools, and we simply couldn't miss out on experiencing a hot sand bath at the Takegawara Onsen, the oldest sand bathing establishment in Beppu.

However, the highlight of a trip to Beppu is undoubtedly the set of seven 'Hells', each of which features different geothermal features — blue water, reddish-brown water, bubbling mud that resembles bald heads poking out of the water, a geyser, a takeaway establishment with foods cooked in thermally-heated water, and, bizarrely, a crocodile park. They were all fascinating, and many of the places had foot baths.

Monkeys

From Beppu we also visited the Umitamago Aquarium and Takasakiyama Monkey Park, which are located on either side of the main road halfway between Beppu and Oita. The aquarium had the usual dolphin/small whale and walrus shows, but also featured a pelican parade and a coral reef feeding show where the diver used an underwater camera to zoom in for close-ups. There was a stunning display of display tanks lit up in a dark room. Like all the aquaria so far, there were some new things that we had never seen before — such as an argonaut (octopus) preserved in the shell that the animal had used as an egg float (we call the shell a 'paper nautilus').

The monkey park was a huge area where two populations of Japanese macaques live in their natural habitat. Visitors are requested not to look them in the eye (perceived as a threat and likely to provoke an attack), feed them (they are fed wheat by the park staff) or hassle them in any way, as they can be vicious despite their small size. Two groups, each of 700–800 members and responding to different calls, come down the mountain alternately to be fed. There was a thick swarm of these small monkeys as hundreds tore down from the mountain when called, and the noise they made was absolutely deafening.

Mochi

The final thing we did before leaving Beppu was a walk along the seafront where we came across an interesting sea wall construction for dampening tsunamis and also a community mochi (rice ball)-making event at the local shrine. A woman walking in the opposite direction at the traffic lights had excitedly alerted us to the latter. The people at the shrine were very welcoming and invited us in to have a go at pounding the rice and stuffing the mochi with red beans. We were extremely lucky to happen upon this once-a-year event!

Above: Hot sand baths, Takegawara Onsen; Below Left: Umi Jigoku, Beppu; Below Right: Onishibouzu Jigoku, Beppu

Super ring, Sand dollars & Subtropical plants
Aso & Aoshima: 29 January–2 February

CHAPTER SIXTEEN

Above: Sunset and view of smoking Mount Aso from street near Guest House Asora

Above: Daikanbo on rim of caldera; Below: Guest House Asora

ASO & AOSHIMA: 29 January–2 February

Super ring

We had visited the area south of Mount Aso (the largest active volcano in the world) a couple of months previously, but decided to visit the north side separately because access between the two sides of Mount Aso wasn't easy or convenient using public transport.

In Aso Town we stayed at the gorgeous Guest House Asora, where the host's first rule is that you must talk to her and the other guests. Her English was as good as our Japanese (i.e. very poor) so it was great practice. The local convenience store sold every kind of fried food imaginable, while the restaurant next door to the supermarket had delicious set lunches of local fare, such as pickle rice and vegetable dumpling soup (choice of wheat or rice flour dumplings), and its ceilings were decorated with an array of hanging ceramic dolls.

One of the attractions at Mount Aso is the 'Aso Super Ring' (so-called 'Rim of Fire'), a somewhat disappointing audio-visual display located at the start of the now closed ropeway to the top of the volcano. We knew that the ropeway was closed (since 2014, due to the dangerous conditions), but it didn't matter because we had been up there in 1992. Afterwards we walked back along the road from the fog-bound Super Ring for about three kilometres to the Volcano Museum in complete whiteout and freezing winds.

The Volcano Museum had an excellent audio-visual show and very comprehensive displays. After viewing the displays, the weather cleared so we could enjoy views of the lakes and the smoking mountain over lunch at the restaurant, before catching the bus back to town. The lunch was a local specialty hot-pot, which was welcome and warming after our walk down the mountain. The next day was sunny and we visited Daikanbo on the rim of the ancient caldera for more spectacular views of Mount Aso. The caldera measures about 24 x 18 kilometres.

While in Aso Town we also visited the two onsens in the town, located between the station and our accommodation, for post-sightseeing relaxation.

Sand dollars

On our way south, we decided to stop off at Aoshima, just south of Miyazaki, to break the journey from Aso in the centre of Kyushu to Kagoshima in the far south. With several changes of train (not a problem in Japan), we arrived at Aoshima town in the late-ish afternoon.

We chose Aoshima on a whim because *Lonely Planet* said there were often sand dollars washed up on the beach after storms. Indeed, the beach was a long and beautiful surf beach with sand dollars every few metres! Sand dollars are flat sea urchins that are very fragile and not worth trying to carry home intact in your luggage!

Subtropical plants

Our Guest House Hooju in Aoshima was basic but in a very handy location for the beach, the Miyako Botanic Garden, and Aoshima itself, a small island 1.5 kilometres in circumference, accessed via a bridge and surrounded by an unusual stepped rock-block geological apron known as the Giant's Washboard or in Japanese 'Oni-no-sentakuita' meaning 'Ogre's Washboard'.

The Botanic Garden had lovely flower bed displays (remember it was the dead of winter in Aoshima at the time), and two superb glasshouse displays. The garden specialises in acclimatising subtropical plant seeds and seedlings donated from Brazil and Argentina.

One of the small glasshouses contained an interesting collection of tropical fruit trees. Inside it reminded us of what we were (not) missing in Sydney — 41˚C and 100% humidity; the outside temperature was around 3˚C, so glasses and phones quickly became fogged over.

We visited one of the local onsens in Aoshima, which turned out to be a bit unusual in having pools with rocks on the bottom as well as single-person urns (in the women's) and cave-like structures (in the men's). Bill had the men's virtually to himself, whereas I shared the women's with the local elderly ladies plus the Gifu women's football team. With six different indoor and outdoor pools, there was plenty of room for everyone!

Photo Page 69: Sand dollar on beach at Aoshima

Above: Aoshima Shrine; Below: Giant's Washboard rock formations, Aoshima Island

CHAPTER SEVENTEEN

Ferry, Farmed shrimp & Flying fish
Yakushima: 4–11 February

Above: Yakushima from ferry; Below: Deep fried flying fish

YAKUSHIMA: 4–11 February

Ferry

We spent a week on the gorgeous island of Yakushima, accessed by a four-hour ferry trip from Kagoshima. A large percentage of the island is National Park and is World Heritage because of its natural attributes. You can drive around the island in about three hours, though there's a dangerous 26 kilometre stretch only open in daylight hours, and there are only two roads into the interior where the mountains reach over 1800 metres and more than 40 are above 1000 metres.

Yakushima's vertical distribution of climate and vegetation mirrors that of Japan — from subtropical (30° latitude) with coral reefs and sandy beaches (where turtles nest) at sea level, to the high mountains which have the same annual average temperature as Sapporo, up to six metres of snow in winter and an annual rainfall of ten metres.

There are around 2000 different species of plants on Yakushima, and there's a very high degree of endemism. There are many cedars over 1000 years of age. Called 'yakusugi', they grow slowly and have tight growth rings and lots of resin. Interestingly Yakushima is a granite island pushed up out of the ocean, whereas the neighbouring island of Kuchinoerabujima, only 12 kilometres away, is an aggregation of 10 active volcanoes. The whole population of the latter was evacuated in 2014 when one of its volcanoes blew up.

There are some serious 12-hour or overnight mountain treks/climbs you can do on Yakushima (disposable toilet bags must be carried), but we opted for two four-hour walks, one to the Yakusugi Land Jomonsugi Cedar and the other to Taikoiwa Rock in the Shiratani Unsuikyo Ravine (a 450 metre climb). Both were beautiful walks, with many cedars to be seen along with deer and macaques, the latter being lighter in colour and more hairy than those on mainland Japan.

Farmed shrimp

We stayed in our own 'Orange House Cottage', a small cottage behind an orange house owned and built by a retired professor of computer science and his artist wife, who were extremely kind and helpful. One day they took us to the local shrimp farm, located between our cottage and the port town of Miyanoura, where we all bought shrimp for dinner.

On a day that promised the best weather we drove right around the island. We had a hire car for the week and were advised to go anticlockwise so that we would be next to the mountain on the dangerous narrow section. We also wanted to arrive at the Hirauchi Kaichu onsen within two hours of low tide. This onsen is a beautiful series of hot pools set at different levels, with the hottest at the top, and the lower ones gradually becoming cooler as the tide comes in. No bathing costumes were allowed, but our host kindly lent me a toweling 'moo-moo' and Bill used his trekking towel.

Flying fish

On wet days we visited various museums and gardens on our own, but one day when the winds were gale force and the rain relentless, our hosts took us on a tour half way around the island and back to show us two spectacular waterfalls (Oko-no-taki and Sanpiro-no-taki), and the four of us enjoyed a lovely lunch — the specialty of the island, deep fried flying fish coated with potato flour — after which we had afternoon tea with an artist friend of theirs and her husband.

We spent extra time on Yakushima because the weather turned nasty — rain, gale force winds, hail, snow and huge seven metre seas meant that the car ferry and all high speed boats were cancelled on the day that we were supposed to return to Kagoshima. We managed to get the last seats on a flight out on the following evening. Not surprisingly, the flight was quite rough. In the meantime a lot of snow had fallen on the mountains, the high waterfalls had frozen and the seas were still over five metres.

We managed to fill in the extra day with a visit to the dentist for Bill (kindly arranged by our host), a lunch of baked flying fish in town, and a visit to the small riverside Kusugawa Onsen. Our hosts didn't charge us for the extra night and the car hire company let us keep the car for the extra day at no further cost.

Above: Steps on track, Yakusugi Land, Yakushima

Above: Giant cedar, Shiratani Unsuikyo; Below: Taikoiwa Rock, Shiratani Unsuikyo

Animatronics, Active volcanoes & Akune
Kagoshima, Izumi & Okayama: 3 & 12–19 February

Above: Sakurajima, view from Sengan-en Garden

Above: Samurai training, Sengan-en Garden, Kagoshima; Below: Crane Observation Centre; Right: Saigo Takamori, Meiji Museum

KAGOSHIMA, IZUMI & OKAYAMA: 3 & 12–19 February

Animatronics

We stayed in the Hotel Remm in Kagoshima before travelling to Yakushima, and afterwards for three nights at an Airbnb in an outer suburb. The Museum of the Meiji Restoration was a highlight — all about the Satsuma Rebellion and consequent industrial and social reforms that started here and spread through the whole of Japan.

The museum had a wonderful presentation with very life-like animatronics that really brought historic figures to life. We also visited Sengan-en, an interesting garden surrounding a samurai villa, with an outlook across the bay to the Sakurajima vulcano. The garden had a 'kyokusui no en' — a stream for poetry parties, where participants had to finish composing a haiku before a floating cup of sake launched by others upstream reached them.

Active volcanoes

A cruise around and across the bay to spend the day on Sakurajima is a must when visiting Kagoshima. Sakurajima is a double volcano with one half currently and constantly active. Children wear helmets to school, there are ash shelters everywhere, and there are constructions on the hillsides to control possible mud and lava flows. The nightly news in Kagoshima features an ash report, so people know whether to hang washing out or not the following day. We watched people using the 100 metre-long hot foot bath, then did a long walk along the coastal lava fields, finishing off the day with a visit to an onsen that boasted water heated by magma.

From Kagoshima we took a shinkansen to Izumi to spend several days and see the largest concentration of over-wintering migratory cranes in Japan, before they headed off to Siberia (seven species, of which three were still present). There was a very informative and modern crane museum, and an observation centre overlooking thousands of birds.

Akune

Other highlights of Izumi were its well-preserved samurai district, where we had our own personalised tours of two samurai houses, and a shrine with the biggest bell in Japan. On the other days we used the Orange Train, a local single carriage train that operates between Satsumasendai and Yatsushiro, and gets its name from the wealth of different types of citrus fruit grown in the area. At the Satsumasendai end we visited a shrine at the top of a mountain and did a long walk, then hopped off the train at Akune on the way home to visit an onsen that featured floating bankan, a type of huge citrus fruit.

We then headed for Okayama, a city we had been to earlier when staying in Kurashiki to visit the lovely garden Koraku-en. We spent Sunday morning strolling around Okayama and watching people playing 'ground golf', after attending the 'Naked Man Festival' or Saidaiji Eyo at the Saidai temple just outside Okayama the previous night.

The Naked Man Festival featured a full schedule of taiko drumming and dancing right through the afternoon and into the night, culminating with the throwing of the 'shingi' or sacred wooden sticks to a crowd of (almost) naked men at 10 pm. From about 7 pm on, groups of boys, then groups of men, in loincloths, snaked their way through the huge crowds, dipping into a pool of cold water on their way to the main stage of the temple. Although the air temperature was 0°C and there was a wind chill and our feet were numb, we were otherwise warmish from being in the crowd.

Naked male participants (around 10,000) have to register with emergency phone number and blood type. They aren't allowed to have tattoos, jewellery or glasses (as participants would be 'exposed to serious danger'), and it's against the rules to drink alcohol if you're a participant. There were many ambulances on standby and the event became scarier and scarier as more and more naked men crowded onto a relatively small area of temple stage. The naked men moved as a mass, spilling down the steep steps in waves, men tumbling on top of each other as more and more tried to get to the platform at the top, while the ones at the bottom tried to shore up the mass of bodies above.

Photo Page 77: Naked Man Festival at Saidai Temple, Okayama

Above: Naked Man Festival, Okayama; Below: Cold water dip, Naked Man Festival

Above: Young participants; Below: Women drummers, Naked Man Festival, Okayama

Mitsu, Miso fish & Morning market
Matsuyama & Uchiko: 20–25 February

Above: Suikinkutsu, Ninomaru Garden; Below: Mitsu port　　Above: Pilgrim at Taisanji Temple

MATSUYAMA & UCHIKO: 20–25 February

Mitsu

Our Airbnb in Matsuyama on Shikoku Island was located in the historic port suburb of Mitsu. The apartment was small and compact, but had everything we needed. Best of all, there were many restaurants nearby, as well as good supermarkets, the fish market, and plenty of historic places to visit.

One day we did the steep walk up to Matsuyama Castle rather than take the cable car or chairlift, and walked down behind the castle to visit the very interesting Ninomaru Historical Garden, where the floor plan of old buildings of one of the baileys is represented in a contemporary layout with a design incorporating water features, citrus trees and flowering shrubs. A beautiful and interesting feature in the garden was a 'suikinkutsu', in which an empty jar is buried upside down, its upturned bottom having a small hole through which water drips into a shallow dish below, and the echo of the dripping produces an exquisite sound when you listen through a bamboo pipe protruding from the ground.

On another day we tried the local dish of 'tai kameshi' (kettle steamed rice with sea bream) for lunch, then visited the Dogo Onsen Honkan, Japan's oldest onsen (3000 years of recorded history) for a nice hot bath. Afterwards we acquainted ourselves with various features in the area — foot spas, Botchan Karaduri Clock, and the Yuzuki Castle ruins.

Matsuyama is famous for its haiku poets and there are many 'haiku boxes' around the city, in which you can deposit your poems in the hope they may get published. One day we stayed at home in Mitsu and I was lucky enough to get an appointment at a dentist a few blocks away for teeth cleaning (the works, including fluoride treatment and someone to translate, all for $30), after which we found a lovely sushi/sashimi restaurant almost next door to our apartment for lunch, then wandered around looking at historic buildings.

Mitsu is one of the few areas where a whole suburb has escaped tragedies like fires, earthquakes, typhoons and tsunamis for many centuries. We took the free ferry, which traverses a whole 80 metres from one side of the port to the other — only to find that the ferry driver was one of the men who had been sitting next to us at lunch in the local restaurant.

Miso fish

We spent another day at Uchiko, a small town an hour away from Matsuyama on the train. There were plenty of things to do there. We visited the Uchiko-za theatre which has performances of kabuki (drama) and bunraku (puppetry), the Museum of Commercial and Domestic Life, the Wax Museum (wax production for candles and cosmetics), the Ikazaki Kite Museum, a lovely covered bridge in the countryside (by taxi), and we walked through a beautifully preserved historic district. The centrepiece of our lunch was a delicious miso-fish dish.

Morning market

Back in Mitsu we spent Saturday morning at the very crowded fish market at the end of our street, where the big Mitsu Morning Market is held on four Saturdays a year — one fortunately coinciding with our visit.

On the weekend before leaving Matsuyama we visited a temple close to where we were staying at Mitsu. Shikoku is well known for its 88-Temple Pilgrimage, and this one (Taisanji) was the first we visited and number 52 on the pilgrimage route. The temple complex was beautiful and there were a couple of pilgrims there, so I asked one if I could photograph him. Next thing I knew the pilgrim was getting us to light candles and incense, pray and ring the bell, and he was telling us about his progress.

He then took us to the office to see his pilgrim's book being annotated (calligraphy, done on the spot) and before we knew it he had bought me a sheet of paper with the same calligraphy on it. He wouldn't accept any payment for the 600 yen cost, and if we had stayed any longer to argue the point we would have missed our bus so I paid it back in 100 yen installments at the donation boxes of the next six temples we visited.

Photo Page 81: History & Folklore Museum, Museum of Commercial & Domestic Life, Uchiko

Above: Uchiko-za, wooden kabuki and puppetry theatre; Below: Covered bridge, Uchiko   Above: Haiku post box

CHAPTER TWENTY

Chicken necks, Camellias & Chinkabashi
Sukumo, Shimanto & Cape Ashizuri: 26–28 February

Above: Display at Dragonfly Kingdom, Shimanto; Below: Curvature of the earth from Cape Ashizuri

Below: Rock garden, Kongofukuji Temple

SUKUMO, SHIMANTO & CAPE ASHIZURI: 26–28 February

Chicken necks

We spent a few days in Sukumo after taking a highway bus from Matsuyama at the beginning of the week. The island of Shikoku is very mountainous and not as well serviced by trains as other parts of Japan.

While in Sukumo, we managed to sample some of the many unusual dishes from the local area, including sushi made with local vegetables (inakazushi), seared bonito sashimi (katsuo no tataki) and baked bonito. The most notable cuisine we sampled in Sukumo was charcoal chicken. We had two dishes — chicken necks and chicken thighs — both of which consisted of chicken seemingly blackened from being coated and/or soaked in charcoal. Surprisingly, the necks were better than the thighs, but neither was particularly attractive or appetising.

Camellias

The highlight of our time in Sukumo was a visit to the south-western cape, Cape Ashizuri (or Ashizuri Mizaki) in a local bus that travelled along the very steep and windy coast on a narrow single-lane road. Needless to say the scenery was spectacular. The road passed through a beautiful 'green tunnel' lined in various places with red flowering camellias.

Cape Ashizuri is the southernmost point of Shikoku Island and is part of the Ashizuri-Uwakai National Park. From a viewing platform at the cape lighthouse there's an amazing 270° panorama of the Pacific Ocean, where the view of the horizon demonstrates, spectacularly, the curvature of the earth. The pathways in the area around the lighthouse were lined with camellia forests and there was also a large subtropical botanical garden to wander through.

Another path led down to the spectacular granite Hakusan Natural Arch, which can also be viewed in comfort from the top of the cliff at the relatively newly built and naturally heated foot spa named after John Manjiro. John Manjiro was born in the area and rescued by an Amerian whaling ship from an uninhabited island after his fishing boat drifted away in a storm. After living in the USA for some time he returned and played a major role in modernising Japan.

There is a Manjiro statue at the entrance to the lighthouse pathway, which leads, in the opposite direction from the foot spa and arch, to an interesting path along the foreshore with a set of signs interpreting shoreline features and ancient stones, stone tools and earthenware that are possibly of neolithic origin. At Cape Ashizuri we also visited Kongofukuji Temple, number 38 on the Shikoku 88-Temple Pilgrimage, which featured pagodas and extensive rock gardens — literally, gardens consisting only of rocks.

Chinkabashi

On the way home from Cape Ashizuri we visited the world's first (and possibly only) dragonfly park at Shimanto, the Tombo Okoku Dragonfly Kingdom. The indoor displays were wonderful. Of course, it wasn't the right season for seeing the actual insects in the surrounding outdoor habitats, so we had to settle for seeing them in all their glorious colours in the indoor photographic display. In summer there are 76 species in the Shimanto area and the outdoor display area features all the various types of habitats to attract them.

The Shimanto River is famous for its many chinkabashi — submersible bridges without handrails, designed to submerge in floods, but unfortunately that day we ran out of time to visit one of them.

We did a lot of walking in Sukumo, including a three-hour walk across a bridge and right around the nearby Oshima Island. It was low tide and there were quite a few locals out on the rock shelves scraping around for shellfish. There was a large amount of fishing paraphernalia around the coastline — nets, floats, boats, and so on — as well as boat-building enterprises and a port on the side of the island facing the mainland.

On Oshima Island there were gardens, many growing food crops, and we walked past mushrooms, beans and fish drying on racks or in netted containers hanging outside in the sun.

Photo Page 85: Farms and Matsuda River from Hotel Avan, Sukumo, at sunrise

Above: View from walk around Oshima Island, Sukumo; Row Below: Food drying racks, Oshima Island

Below: Boat building, Oshima Island

Yuji, Yakatabune & Yuzu
Kochi & Niyodo: 1–5 March

Above: Fish, Kochi Sunday Market; Below: Sculpted apple at food ikebana display, Kochi

KOCHI & NIYODO: 1–5 March

Yuji

We stayed in Kochi for a week at a lovely Airbnb that was an entire old house, with owner Yuji and gorgeous dog Kuli living next door. We were our host's first 'foreign' guests at the Airbnb. We particularly loved using the beautiful crockery that was supplied in the Airbnb, along with the huge amount of space — we counted around 30 doorways, some of which had more than one sliding door.

There was plenty to do in Kochi. On Thursday we used the 'city tour' bus to visit Katsurahama Beach, with its white sands and beautiful pine trees. We walked around and saw the statue of Sakamoto Ryoma, but decided to pass on the Sakamoto Ryoma Memorial Museum on the hill, the aquarium and the Tosa Dog Park.

On another day we visited the Chikurinji Temple (number 31 along the Shikoku 88-Temple Pilgrimage) and the Makino Botanical Garden. The Makino Botanical Garden was very colourful despite it being winter. It had a very modern and comprehensive 'Plants and People' exhibition hall (with lovely botanically-inspired lights), and a conservatory with the best display of orchids we had ever seen, as well as the usual suspects — jade vine, heliconias, palms, amazon lilies and carnivorous plants. The display was simply stunning and probably reflects the Garden's close association with Singapore Botanic Gardens.

Yakatabune

One of the highlights of the wider Kochi area was a houseboat cruise we did along the Niyodo River. The houseboat ('yakatabune') was very low in the water, with everyone sitting, somewhat uncomfortably, on floor cushions with scant headroom. When the windows were opened occasionally for taking photos (it was too cold to leave them open), we seemed to be sitting almost at water level. The river scenery was beautiful and we saw an eagle or two along the way.

The meeting point for the cruise was a building on the riverbank, where fish were being dried using big fans, barbecues were set up for cooking fish, and there was a very lovable pet wild boar called Tombo-chan. After the cruise, the man from the houseboat company kindly arranged for us to get a lift back as far as Tosawashi Kogeimura 'Qraud', from where we could more easily catch a bus back to Kochi. The driver took us a different way from the way we had come, via one of the chinkabashi submersible bridges that the Niyodo and Shimanto Rivers are famous for, and which we hadn't time to see in Shimanto. With no classes being held that day at Qraud — a traditional Japanese paper-making workshop — we were able to wander through the classrooms as well as the shop.

Yuzu

We visited Kochi Castle and enjoyed the lovely gardens surrounding the castle buildings. On our last day in Kochi we visited the 300-year-old Sunday Market, which was huge and brim-full of the most interesting things to buy, as well as many delicious things to eat and drink. Market stalls stretch for many blocks over a distance of about 1.3 kilometres, and this open-air, all-day market is the largest of its kind in Japan, attracting about 15,000 shoppers every week.

We sampled some of the street food, including tempura sweet potato and a yuzu-filled sweet pikelet (yuzu is a citrus half way between lime and lemon in taste) and grilled sweet potato snacks. There was everything from street food, fresh fruit and vegetables grown by local farmers, plants, flowers, hardware and clothes, to knives and antiques — and the market wasn't at all repetitive or boring.

There was also a whole arcade filled with an exhibition of 'food ikebana', which was simply stunning. The following Sunday the same arcade was going to be filled with trestle tables for an all-day sake-drinking event called 'Tosa no Ikyaku'.

We left Kochi (and our Airbnb's gorgeous dog) on Monday, and took two trains through the centre of Shikoku to the large city of Tokushima on the north-east coast. Getting transport the long way around via the coast would simply have been too difficult.

Above: Driving across a chinkabashi submersible bridge

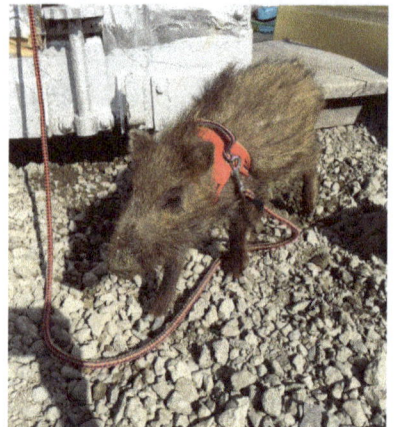
Above: Tombo-chan; Below: Yakatabune, Niyodo River

Above: Niyoda River

Pilgrims, Pacific & Pools
Cape Muroto & Tokushima: 4 & 6–11 March

Above: Pilgrim shop; Below Left: Egg-vending machine; Below Right: Statue of Shintaro Nakaoka, Cape Muroto

CAPE MUROTO & TOKUSHIMA: 4 & 6–11 March

Pilgrims

While in Kochi we did a day trip by bus to the eastern cape, Cape Muroto (or Muroto Mizaki), and the nearby Hotsumisaki Temple (number 24 on the Shikoku 88-temple pilgrimage). The Shikoku coastline around the cape is superb, with spectacular cliffs and many small islands. It would have been nice to stay at the cape on the way to Tokushima, but the distances were too great and it was easier to travel to Tokushima via the inland rail line.

Our Airbnb apartment in Tokushima was almost right at the station and, though compact, was very comfortable and cozy. Not that we were home very much as there was a lot to do.

On the first day in Tokushima we visited the first five temples (numbers one to five) of the 88-temple pilgrimage. We did it as much to enjoy the walk as to visit the temples, because they are all located within a ten-kilometre stretch and we were in training for our eleven-day Nakasendo walk in a few weeks' time. The temple walk passed through small towns and rural areas (where we came across an egg-vending machine), so it was both interesting and quiet. We travelled along many back roads alongside the real pilgrims, who were spending a couple of months walking right around Shikoku to visit all 88 temples. We also encountered a tour group of more time-strapped or elderly pilgrims who were travelling by bus. Temple number 1 was interesting because it is the main place for enrolling as an 'O-henro' pilgrim and for buying the gear — hat, staff, jacket, bag, maps and books.

Pacific

On another day we took the train down the coast as far as Mugi, where the 'Mollusco Mugi' houses a collection of around 2500 shells in a beautiful mollusc-shaped building right on the Pacific sea-shore. Sadly the live nautiluses promised in *Lonely Planet* seemed to have met their demise as there were no living molluscs and the price had dropped to half that listed in the book.

One useful thing about travelling in Japan is that prices generally reflect value. So if you're paying 200 yen, 500 yen or 1000 yen entry to a museum or for food, you know what to expect. Also useful to know is that food at restaurants located at tourist venues doesn't usually cost more than you would pay for the same food elsewhere. What more could you ask for? — value for money, no tourist rip-offs, and no tipping!

Pools

One day we travelled out to Naruto on a local bus to see the whirlpools under the Onaruto Bridge. Best viewed at particularly high or low tides, huge whirlpools form due to the very strong currents. We were there at low tide, when the whirlpools form on the Pacific side, whereas at high tide they form on the Inland Sea side. There's a 450 metre walkway underneath the bridge with wire mesh along the sides, so that you can feel the power of the wind, and glass panels in both the floor and at the sides at regular intervals. The pedestrian flow was one-way, typical of Japanese efficiency in managing large numbers of people.

There were many seaweed farms in this area, and we saw people harvesting seaweed from small boats and processing it on shore. Unfortunately we were on the bus, so we couldn't get a good close-up look at the proceedings. On our way home from Naruto (about an hour away) we took the 20-minute boat tour around the city centre island, under 18 very low bridges and past the Central Park with its cherry blossoms in full bloom. The boat ride was free except for a 200 yen insurance payment.

On our way home through the city we went to the Awa Odori Dance show, a very lively, informative and entertaining show which unfortunately (for Bill) included audience participation. Needless to say, they couldn't get him to budge from his seat, while I made the effort and won a certificate and scarf — probably because I was the only non-Japanese person dancing rather than for my dancing ability, and I got to answer a couple of fortunately easy questions in Japanese when accepting the awards.

Photo Page 93: Pilgrim walking sticks, Jizoji Temple number 5 on Shikoku 88-Temple Pilgrimage

Above: Onaruto Bridge; Below: Naruto whirlpools

Below: Anime characters at Tokushima Castle

Above: Awa Odori dance show, Tokushima

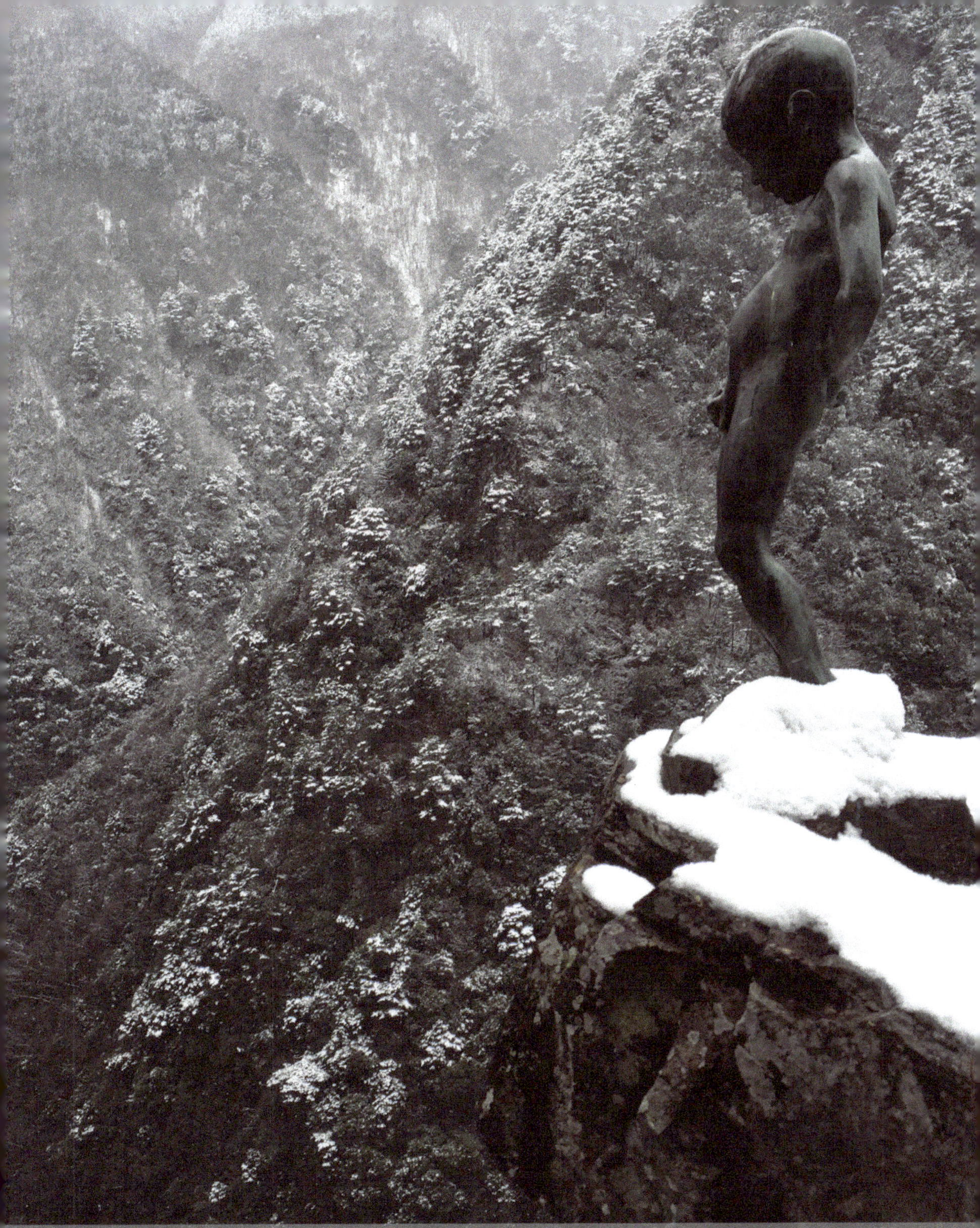

Snow, Sightseeing train & Sand spit
Iya Valley & Miyazu: 8 & 12–15 March

Above: Kazura-bashi vine bridge, Nishi-Iya

Above: Kazura-bashi vine bridge, Nishi-Iya; Below: Sightseeing train Kyoto to Amanohashidate

Above: Woman farmer with NASA jacket, Miyamura

IYA VALLEY & MIYAZU: 8 & 12–15 March

Snow

We were keen to visit the Iya Valley and had booked to stay at Chiourii (of *Lost Japan* fame). However we had to cancel when told that four-wheel drive and chains were required because winter lasted longer in the valley and the roads were steep and treacherous.

Instead, we caught the train from Tokushima and did a one-day trip into the Iya Valley, having booked a two-hour taxi tour starting from Obuke station. Despite the weather being fine for weeks prior, it snowed all the way into the valley, and we were glad not to be driving ourselves yet still get to see the main sights: the 'Peeing Boy' statue, the nearby Hotel Nanoyado with a cablecar down to its onsen on the river (at the time the cablecar was halfway down the hill), the Heike Folklore House, the Kazura-bashi (vine bridge), and the Biwa-no-take waterfall. The vine bridge at Nishi-Iya is one of only three remaining and was particularly slippery and scary after the snowfall. Everyone but Bill was hanging on with both hands and inching their way across. Vine bridges were built so they could be slashed when the enemy was approaching. Stalls near the bridge were selling delicious-smelling skewered fish and vegetables cooked over hot coals — just the thing for a cold snowy day.

Sightseeing train

At the end of our stay in Tokushima on Shikoku we travelled all day by various trains, including Bill's favourite — the shinkansen — to reach Miyamura Station and our Airbnb at Miyazu on the Sea of Japan coast of Honshu (Kyoto Prefecture).

We hadn't checked the tickets when we bought them and found that we had been sold tickets for a later shinkansen than we requested, possibly because the one we wanted was full. We only had nine minutes after getting off the shinkansen to negotiate our way to platform number 31 in Kyoto Station (where we had never been before). It took us 9.5 minutes, and our rapid express had just pulled out as we ran onto the platform. Then we had to wait an hour for the next train and forgo our reserved seats. This actually turned out to be quite fortunate as the final local train just happened to be the afternoon tourist train, a single carriage with cafe and table seating.

We went to Miyazu because there was little accommodation on the Sea of Japan coast. However we struck it lucky as the Airbnb we stayed in for four nights turned out to be a gorgeous old traditional-style mud and timber construction house in a little country village, set amongst vegetable fields. The place, called the 'Coco House', had a nice modern bathroom and good cooking facilities, with really lovely crockery (one of the joys of many Japanese kitchens). The bedroom was in the loft, where two very comfortable beds were laid out on the floor, with windows overlooking neighbouring roofs, and a straw ceiling. One night it snowed, so we woke up to a view of snowy white roofs and trees. Miyazu was very cold but the house was cosy with a kerosene heater downstairs and AC upstairs. We could easily have stayed a lot longer in that house!

Sand spit

Unbeknown to us when we booked our accommodation in Miyazu, one of Japan's 'top three most beautiful sights' was only just down the road — Amanohashidate, a 3.6 kilometre long sand spit with natural pine forest lining a gravel road, and apparently a summer delight for picnics, swimming and cycling, with an amusement park at one end and cablecars/chairlifts at both ends. Together with a few temples, restaurants and onsens, you've got a huge tourist attraction. We did a recce on the day after we arrived, by walking several kilometres to town and back to check the place out.

The following day — the only day when the weather forecast was favourable — we took two of the Airbnb bicycles and spent the day riding to the coast and across the Amanohashidate sand spit and back. Despite the freezing weather, the sand spit was beautiful, there was an interesting opening bridge with coal barges passing through just as we got there, and wild rugosa roses were growing in one part of the pine forest.

Above: Amanohashidate from Kasamatsu Park

Above: Opening bridge, Amanohashidate; Below: Barge passing through opened bridge, Amanohashidate

Tori, Tulips & Temples
Kyoto: 16–23 March

CHAPTER TWENTY-FOUR

101

Above: Fushimi-Inari Shrine: Below Left: Path to summit of Mount Inari; Below Right: Tsutenkyo Bridge Garden, Kyoto

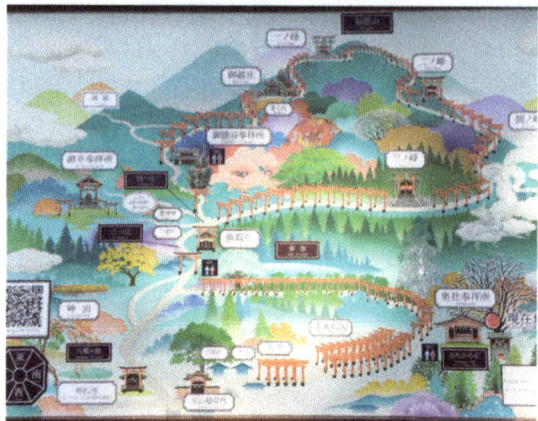

Below: Kyoto Railway Museum

KYOTO: 16–23 March

Tori

We arrived in Kyoto on a Thursday and spent the Friday on a walk that took in Trip Advisor's number one most popular tourist attraction in Japan — the Fushimi-Inari Shrine, with thousands of vermillion tori gates that feature in almost every brochure on Japan, along with many statues of 'inari' (foxes).

Luckily we arrived early and were able to get a few photos without people in them — by the time we left, the crowds were enormous. We've since been told that this time of year in Kyoto is not only chock-a-block with tourists here for the cherry blossoms, but also that it's also the end of the high school and university years — so it's a bit like the Australian 'schoolies' week. Our walk after Fushimi-Inari took in two important temples (Tofukuji and Sennyuji) and two gorgeous temple gardens (Hojo Garden and Tsutenkyo Bridge Garden).

We stayed in K's House Hostel Kyoto, which is cheap and friendly with small, clean, comfortable bedrooms with ensuite, and large lounge areas and kitchen facilities. We had become used to seeing mainly Japanese tourists on our travels so far — hardly any 'gaijin' or foreigners — so it was a bit of a shock to come to a city full of American, European, South American, British and Aussie tourists, as well as Japanese, Chinese, Taiwanese and Koreans.

That said, it was obvious that people from all over the world want to come to Japan, and Kyoto in particular, for 'hanami' — plum and cherry blossom viewing time. We had been following the blooming, from when it began in the Yaeyama Islands in January, to the rest of Okinawa, Kyushu and Shikoku in February, to Honshu in March. Now the plums were looking good in Kyoto, and in a week's time the cherries would be fully out and looking their very best.

Tulips

Spring was in the air and many other plants were blooming besides plums and cherries. We saw the first red rhododendron and a couple of yellow irises. Tulips and other bulbs were in flower too. But it was the cherry blossoms that were taking the limelight, both real ones and the fake ones decorating department stores. The nighttime light show in the castle grounds was about to start, as was the light show at the Toji Temple — the latter to be powered by zero-emission car technology.

Many young tourists had hired kimonos and were heading out into the streets, temples and parks — though some might have been disappointed to have booked their attire for days that turned out to be very cold or very rainy. It's about $50 or so to hire the gear (accessories included) for a few hours of strolling and selfie-taking. We noticed that some kimono-wearers were going slowly, seemingly having trouble getting around on the 'geta' (wooden shoes)!

Temples

In only a matter of days we found we had worked our way through more than half of the walks in our *Kyoto & Vicinity Walking Guide* — a booklet of 24 selected courses that we acquired from the Japan National Tourism Organisation in Sydney — and we'd lost count of how many temples we'd seen. Each one had been different and interesting. Some had been amazing and we were looking forward to visiting even more!

The main temples we had by now visited in Kyoto were Tofukuji, Sennyuji, Ginkakuji (Silver Temple) and Nanzenji. Even though we vowed not to visit any more castles, we went to Kyoto (Nijo-jo) Castle one day and found it to be quite different from the others we had already seen. Of particular interest were the 'nightingale' floorboards, which make a beautiful sound when walked upon and were actually designed for hearing intruders approaching.

We visited the relatively new JR (Japan Rail) Railway Museum with its many steam locos, and the Lake Biwa Aqueduct and its Museum. We also took a stroll along the beautiful and peaceful Philosopher's Walk. There are many shops, cafes and seats for contemplation along the Walk, which follows a small waterway lined with cherry blossoms (unfortunately not yet in flower).

Photo Page 101: Northern Garden, Tofukuji Temple, Kyoto

Above: Viaduct, Nanzenji Temple, Kyoto; Below: Philosopher's Walk, Kyoto   Above: Kimono hire, Kyoto

Gardens, Golden temple & Geisha
Kyoto: 24–30 March

Above & Below: Kinkakuji, Golden Temple, Kyoto

Below Left: Bamboo Path, Arashiyama; Below Right: Door, Imperial Palace, Kyoto

KYOTO: 24–30 March

Gardens

We did the 'hard yards' over our two weeks in and around Kyoto, completing most of the walks in our *Kyoto & Vicinity Walking Guide* booklet of 24 selected courses that we obtained from the Japan National Tourism Organisation in Sydney. Not bad, considering that most of the half-day courses actually took a full day. Admittedly we had already done many of the out-of-town walking courses.

We spent some time in the gardens around the Imperial Palace and Kyoto Castle and in the Shosei-en Garden. At this time of year you can visit the Imperial Palace without a reservation and, while security is strict, it was well worth the effort to see the beautiful buildings and gardens.

One day we visited Toji Temple, with its five-story pagoda (though hard to photograph with all the lighting infrastructure in place for the coming weekend light shows when the cherry blossoms would be at their best). The halls were beautiful inside, with lovely lights and crammed full of chairs for big services/functions/meetings.

Just down the road from the temple was an Indian restaurant for a welcome 'lunch special', though sadly they didn't seem to do 'ladies lunch specials' in Kyoto. An Indian ladies lunch special is about $10 for a set meal of two curries, naan bread, rice, salad, soup and lassi (or soft drink, sometimes even beer).

Golden temple

No trip to Kyoto would be complete without a visit to Kinkakuji, the Golden Temple, and the Rock Garden at Ryoanji. We had visited both before but they were just as beautiful. Even though the Golden Temple was very crowded, the pedestrian traffic was organised in a one-way system that worked extremely well and made the visit seem very relaxing.

Not so for the Arashiyama Hills Bamboo Path which we also visited. We expected a quiet and peaceful stroll through a bamboo forest. It wasn't even mentioned in our book, but it just sounded attractive. However it was literally jam-packed with people walking shoulder-to-shoulder, as well people taking rickshaws rides. We simply couldn't believe the crowds, though the bamboo forest itself was impressive just the same.

On other days we visited the Higashi Honganji and Nishi Honganji Temples near Kyoto Station, and the Sanjusangendo Temple, which has the longest timber temple building in Japan and a display of 1001 statues of Kannon (no photos allowed!) and which was close to our accommodation at our excellent K's House Hostel. We went to Pontocho that night, intending to have dinner, but found it to be very touristy and pricey with 500 yen per person cover charge at most restaurants. So we ended up having a very good and reasonably priced meal at a Thai restaurant, of which there are quite a few in Kyoto.

Geisha

Our final half-day outing from the booklet turned out to be one of the best, when we took the Keihan Railway then the lovely two-car Eizen Railway out to Kurama in the hills for a lovely walk/climb through the forest, viewing various shrines and temples along the way. We rang every bell at every shrine and temple after reading a notice saying that black bears were in the area and the noise of the bells would scare them away. The walk was beautiful, very peaceful and uncrowded. It finished in a lovely (but pricey) little town from where you could walk a couple of kilometres down to catch the return train from a different railway station.

On our final night we met up with the group for our Nakasendo Way walk, which was to start the following morning and end in Tokyo in ten days' time. After the briefing we took taxis to the entertainment district for a sumptuous Japanese dinner at an izakaya restaurant (eating and drinking party restaurant), followed by a stroll through the Gion Geisha district hoping to see a Geisha arriving or leaving by taxi. We were fortunate enough to see an apprentice Geisha (similar in appearance to an actual Geisha but without the vivid white face make-up).

Photo Page 105: Young couple in kimono, Kyoto

Above: Cycads with protective covers, Kyoto Castle

Above: Water buckets for extinguishing fires, Toji Temple; Below: Sanjusangendo Hall, Kyoto

Seismic isolation, Stepping stones & Sculptures
Nara & Kobe: 22 & 27 March

Above: Kasuga Taisha Shrine, Nara; Below: Isuien Garden borrowed scenery, Nara

NARA & KOBE: 22 & 27 March

Seismic isolation

One day during our sojourn in Kyoto we took a train from Kyoto to Nara (about an hour away) where we walked all day to see yet more temples, shrines and gardens. There are no less than eight UNSECO World Heritage listed sites in Nara. The most impressive temple is Todaiji, which houses the 500 tonne, 15 metre tall Daibutsu, or Great Buddha, as well as many smaller buddhas.

Among the many more temples and shrines we visited, the Kofukuji Temple complex, which comprises many beautiful buildings, was also very impressive. The Kofukuji Natural Treasure Hall, part of this complex, was being completely reconstructed. In Japan many important temples and shrines are reconstructed every 20 or 30 years. Often the new building goes up on an adjoining plot of land. The new buildings are partly funded by the donations made by worshippers. Nearly everyone who prays at a temple or shrine throws some money into the box as part of the ritual, and a lot of money is collected from the thousands of small coin donations. The procedure of rebuilding temples and shrines helps to keep ancient building skills alive.

All the temples in Nara were interesting and beautiful, and the gardens were particularly pleasant and peaceful as they were away from the crowds and the hordes of deer — we opted not to buy 'shika-no-fun' or deer biscuits to feed them. Another interesting place to visit in Nara was the Okumura Museum, where you could experience simulations of three of Japan's worst earthquakes.

Stepping stones

We visited two superb gardens adjoining each other, the Isuien Garden and Yoshikien Garden. The former had an interesting use of 'borrowed scenery', incorporating a view to Todaiji Temple in the distance behind a hill within the garden in the foreground. There were interesting features in these gardens, such as walkways with stepping stones, pretty ponds, a water wheel and thatched buildings. Our walk back to Nara Station took us via Wakakusayama Hill and the fabulous Kasuga Taisha Shrine with its large variety of moss-covered stone lanterns.

A week later we set off on an early rapid service train from Kyoto for another trip to spend the day in Kobe. We thought we would have a relaxing hour on the train but it turned out to be jam-packed with people commuting to work in Osaka. We eventually managed to get seats, but only for the short section from Osaka to Kobe.

Sculptures

Kobe is a relatively small port city, very cosmopolitan with a long history of western settlement because it used to be a trading hub in the early days. There is a whole area known as the 'Foreign Settlement Area', which has western-style buildings that house companies such as Lloyds. There is also a lovely garden, the Soraku-en Garden, which has some western buildings and also features the top section of an old regal barge nestled half in and half out of a lake.

Kobe has a bustling Chinatown, where we saw the colourful Chinese Kantel-byo Mausoleum. Just down the road was the more modern but rather drab Indian Honganji Kobe Betsuin Temple. After walking down Flower Road, which features, amongst the many flower beds, a memorial to the 1995 earthquake victims, we visited the ultra-modern Meriken Park Earthquake Memorial Park and Harbor Land on the waterfront. There was a stunning big fish sculpture designed by Canadian-American architect Frank Gehry with installation assistance from Tadao Ando, and an impressive Maritime Museum building (unfortunately closed on Mondays).

The initial part of our walk took us into the hills behind the city, where there were some interesting features including an old elephant enclosure, and a loop road called 'Venus Bridge' which had an expansive view over the city. On both days we lunched at western style cafes — 'Rough Rare' in Kobe (for a delicious meal of roast chicken and vegetables) and 'Monsieur Pepe' in Nara (for a paella). Both these cities are excellent for walking, with English-speaking volunteer guides available in Nara if desired.

Photo Page 109: Statue and clock showing time of Kobe earthquake in 1995, Higashi-Yuenchi Park, Kobe

Above: Flower Road park, Kobe; Below: Chinese Kantei-byo Mausoleum, Kobe

Above: Penny warrior, Kobe

CHAPTER TWENTY-SEVEN

Bear bells, Bananas & Blowfish
Nakasendo Way: 31 March–9 April

Above: Former battlefield, Sekigahara

Above: Sign along path to Sekigahara; Below: School English club, Sekigahara

Above: Hikone Castle

NAKASENDO WAY: 31 March–9 April

Bear bells

The Nakasendo Way walk was excellent, and included many historical features of Japan's Edo period (1603–1868). We walked for ten days along selected parts of the Nakasendo Way, which is the old Edo road inland from Kyoto to Tokyo. Fortunately we didn't encounter any bears. We liked to think that ringing the bear bells along the way scared them off!

We travelled on several trains and buses at various times, but each day's walk (between eight and twenty-four kilometres) was chosen to incorporate important events or historical features such as paths, landscapes, accommodation and post-towns relevant to the Edo period. Post-towns were towns that provided food, accommodation and porters for official travellers and thus helped the shogunate control the road. Our guides were very knowledgeable and we stopped frequently for talks and photo opportunities. As a consequence we learned an enormous amount about Japanese history, culture and religion along the way.

Bananas

The places we visited included Hikone (with an interesting castle), Sekigahara (site of a decisive battle that ended a century of civil wars and opened Japan up to western trade in 1858 and where we were met and entertained by the local school's English Club), Mitake post-town (with a local festival where we lunched on sushi and chocolate bananas), Hosokute post-town (with, nearby, the longest continuous stretch of original ishidatami rock paving in Japan), Okute post-town, Ena (where we visited an exhibition of Hiroshige Edo wood-block prints at the print museum), Nakatsugawa (a prosperous rural town and former post-town), Ochiai post-town, Shinchaya (an inn where we clattered up a large hill in traditional gowns and geta footwear to view the sunset), Magome post-town (where most tourists get dropped off at the top of the steep hill to walk down through the town), Tsumago (the most well-preserved and gorgeous post-town of all), Nagiso (with an impressive wooden suspension bridge), Kiso-Fukushima (where we visited a reconstructed barrier station), the Kaida Plateau (overlooking the active volcano Mount Ontake), Narai post-town, and Karuizawa post-town.

In the final three days we climbed over a number of high passes where there was still a considerable amount of snow (knee deep in places) and ice. We had cleats on our boots to prevent slipping, so the walking was pleasant, despite rain on two days. One day, after climbing over the Jizo Pass through snow, we were treated to a surprise lunch of pizzas and beer in a little restaurant at the base of the Kaida Kogen (Plateau), with the hosts providing musical entertainment as well as a meal, and after which we visited a Kaida horse-breeding stable.

On the final day we walked for about 16 kilometres through maple forest in the rain, snow and ice, up and over the Usui Toge Pass to Yokokawa. The last few kilometres of the three-hour descent were along the disused track-bed of a cog railway. From Yokokawa we travelled by rapid train, then shinkansen, to Tokyo Station where we caught a local train back one station in order to walk the last kilometre of the Nakasendo Way and finish at the Nihonbashi Bridge. Then it was another kilometre or so via Sakura Street (Cherry Blossom Street) near Tokyo Station to our hotel and dinner celebration in the Ginza.

Blowfish

Accommodation along the walk was generally in Japanese inns (ryokans). As the walk progressed the facilities and meals improved, from the first rustic inn where we took turns to use the one communal bath, to luxurious inns with ensuites and onsens. Lunches were generally picnics with food bought in small shops along the way, while breakfasts and dinners were generally quite lavish with interesting local dishes and ingredients — including a clay hot-pot meal, mountain vegetable dishes and freshwater sweet fish. At the final inn we were served with blowfish sashimi, fortunately with no tragic results. And yes, finally, the cherry blossoms were in full bloom when we reached Tokyo!

Above: Torii Toge Pass; Below: Walking through snow on high pass

116

Azaleas, Animal cafes & Antiques
Tokyo: 10–20 April

Above: Cherry blossoms, Sumida Park

Above: Drum Museum; Below: Luggage Museum, Asakusa

Above: Calligrapher working on lanterns

TOKYO: 10–20 April

Azeleas

After completing the Nakasendo Way walk we spent the final night and farewell dinner in the Ginza, after which we moved to K's House Tokyo in Kuramae. We returned to the Ginza the next afternoon to meet up with friends from Sydney and queue up for single-act Kabuki tickets for an evening performance at the beautiful Kabukiza theatre. After the show we had an enjoyable dinner together in the restaurant district under the elevated railway tracks of Yurakucho.

Spring had definitely sprung in Tokyo. One day we walked the six kilometres or so around the outside of the Imperial Palace and spent several hours in the Imperial Palace East Gardens. These Gardens are extensive with swathes of azaleas, lawns, bamboo grove, tea garden, rose garden, iris garden, plum tree grove, and naturalistic areas of woodland and wildflowers. This year the cherry blossom blooming in Honshu was around two weeks later than normal. We had expected to be in Kyoto for the event, or even on the Nakasendo Way, but it didn't happen until we reached Tokyo. In Ueno Park the cherry blossom viewing was in full swing. Our romantic idea of picnics under the cherry blossoms was somewhat quashed when we saw the reality — marked bays on concrete specifying a maximum of ten people allowed per bay, bring-your-own blue tarpaulin, big bins covered in green plastic, scaffold, and big signs specifying all the things you weren't allowed to do (especially no touching of the cherry blossoms).

By contrast, the following day we visited Sumida Park where there were very few people. There was a bit of a breeze, so the ground was covered with fallen petals, and small groups sat picnicking on the grass under huge cherry trees with petals falling on them as if in a snow storm. Just the romantic scene we had imagined!

Animal cafes

Everywhere we went in Japan there seemed to be an unusual cafe or museum. We encountered many cafes in Tokyo where you could have a 'cuppa' or a beer with a bunch of owls or other animals. One day we came across the World Bags and Luggage Museum (free entry and fabulous) and another day the Drum Museum (drums from around the world, and you could have a go at most of them).

In the Kuramae-Asakusa area we were shown a restaurant that specialises in eel and whale dishes (we decided to avoid it!); we visited Orange Street with its handprints of famous actors and singers; we saw a man hand painting calligraphy onto lanterns (we had wondered why they were so expensive); and we wandered along the Sumida River to Ryogoku to visit the Sumo Stadium (Ryogoku Kokugikan) Museum, and to visit the fabulous Tokyo Metropolitan Edo-Tokyo Museum. Did you know that the first mass-produced car in Japan was a Subaru 360?

We also visited Big B shoe shop, which is definitely a must for men with large feet and almost worth a special trip to Tokyo.

We went hiking at Mount Takao on another day (about 50 kilometres out of Tokyo), hoping to get away from the crowds at the city attractions. Alas, there were tens of thousands of people. We took a chairlift halfway up the mountain, then walked to the top (599 metres) via the Takaosan Yakuoin Temple, before hiking 3.2 kilometres down the mountain along a forest path that followed a stream. Back at the station we noticed a Trick Art Museum close by, but it was late in the day so we gave it a miss.

Antiques

On another day we spent several hours wandering around the bi-monthly antiques market at the Tokyo International Forum building, then visited the Marunouchi side of Tokyo Station, to see some of Tokyo's wonderful modern architecture. Surprisingly, Tokyo seemed rather quiet. When we arrived on a Sunday evening, the Ginza had been relatively uncrowded because (we found out later) the main streets were closed to traffic after midday on weekends. Even on a weekday, the Tokyo traffic looked sparse when viewed from Tokyo Skytree, the world's tallest tower — probably because so many people use trains to get around this huge city.

Photo Page 117: International Forum building, Tokyo

Above: Antiques market, International Forum building, Tokyo; Below: Mount Takao

Above: Tokyo Station

Above: Outside owl cafe

Parades, Pandas & Parasitology
Tokyo: 21–30 April

 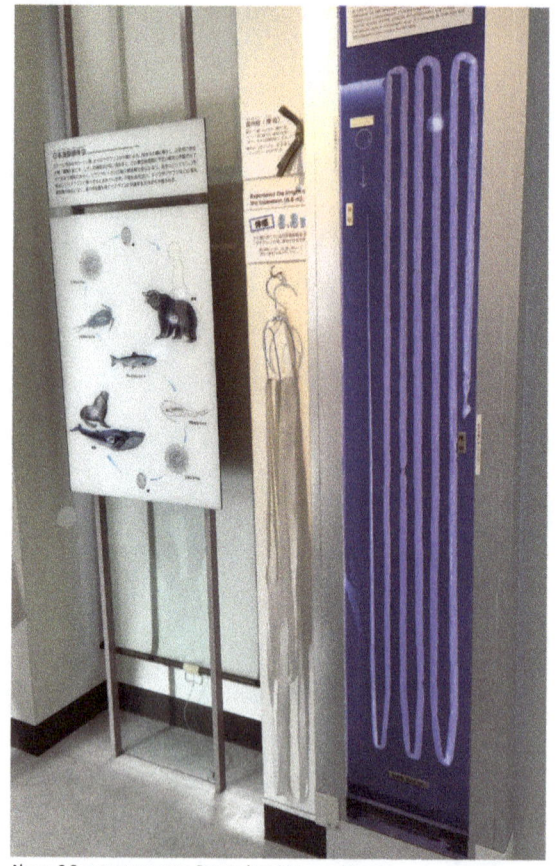

Above: Shop in Kappabashi Street; Below: Institute for Nature Study, Magano   Above: 8.8 metre tapeworm, Parasitology Museum, Magano

TOKYO: 21–30 April

Parades

During the week, we moved from K's House Tokyo in Kuramae to K's House Tokyo Oasis, 1.5 kilometres away in Asakusa. Both hostels are located in very lively and interesting areas full of tourists, souvenir shops, frequent street parades and performances, and many owl and jungle cafes where you can sit and have a drink with one or more different types of birds and/or other animals.

Sensoji Temple, the oldest temple in Tokyo (originally built in 628, rebuilt several times after fires) and its Kaminarimon Gate with huge lantern, were just down the road from our accommodation. In the midst of the Sensoji Temple area was the beautiful Edo period Denboin Garden, which was lovely and peaceful (probably because there was an entry fee!) but only open for two months of the year. When we visited, there was a fascinating indoor exhibition of 'ema', huge old wooden plaques made using a variety of drawing techniques and materials.

Pandas

One day we had lunch in Hibiya Park amidst a large display of tulips, then spent the rest of the day at Ueno Zoo. Although the Zoo is Japan's oldest and many enclosures are far too small, the animals seemed to be well cared for.

The main attractions at Ueno Zoo are the two pandas, which just happened to be located at the furthest point from where we entered the zoo. This actually turned out to be quite fortunate, as the queues had long since gone by the time we reached the pandas just before the zoo closed (though we could see the queue barriers still in place).

We were able to watch the pandas as they enthusiastically romped into their nighttime accommodation area to munch on fresh bamboo and fruit. We were probably luckier than early visitors, judging by the signs warning that pandas spend a lot of time asleep.

We were late reaching the pandas because the zoo was not only much larger than we expected it to be, but because it had so many unusual and interesting animals (ever heard of okapi or fossa?). The bird collection was particularly impressive. However there were very few Australian animals at all — just a few kangaroos, an emu and an echidna. Sadly, they were housed in rather small enclosures.

Parasitology

On our second last day in Tokyo we caught a train to Sunshine City to visit the Sunshine Aquarium that we had been to in 1992. It's located on the 10th floor of a huge shopping centre, along with a planetarium. The displays were good and included live adult and larval nautiluses. One of the shows featured a diver hugging a zebra shark that had a body longer than hers!

On our last day at K's House we visited the Tokyo Institute for Nature Study in Magano. This huge area of natural forest was set aside in 1949 for the study of the plants and animals of the Tokyo area. With only 300 people allowed in at once, it was probably the least crowded part of Tokyo that day. Bill was a hit for spotting a two-metre long snake sitting in a tree, which drew a crowd of photographers. After that, who couldn't resist a visit to the Parasitology Museum down the road to view their 8.8 metre tapeworm?

Other highlights of the week included a day visiting Tokyo Midtown and Roppongi Hills, which are modern high-rise shopping, arts and entertainment developments; the National Art Centre; the Tokyo National Museum at Ueno, followed by a walk through the Yanaka cemetery area, Yanaka Ginza and the Nezu Shrine where the azalea festival was on for a couple of weeks; the National Museum of Modern Art and its Crafts annex, which had a beautiful display of animals in craft; and a visit to Tsukuji.

The Tsukuji Fish Market (now moved to a new location) was huge, with every type of fish and shellfish available. The public was only allowed into the market after 10 am, apart from two batches of 50 people allowed into the 5 am tuna auction (the queue for these tickets started at about 3 or 4 am so we decided not to bother). We also walked up and back along the length of Kappabashi, Tokyo's best-known cooking equipment and utensil street.

Photo Page 121: Whale on the menu in Asakusa street

Above: Tulips in Hibiya Park, Tokyo

Above: Sensoji Temple at night, Asakusa; Below: Diver hugging shark, Sunshine Aquarium, Ikebukuro   Above: Street dancers, Asakusa

CHAPTER THIRTY

Whiskey, Wedding couple & Wisteria
Yokohama, Hitachi & Ashikaga: 23 & 27 April

Above & Below Left: Baseball, Yokohama Stadium; Below Right: Garden Necklace display, Yokohama

Below: Wisterias, Ashikaga Flower Park

YOKOHAMA, HITACHI & ASHIKAGA: 23 & 27 April

Whiskey

One day while staying in Tokyo we went to Yokohama for the day (an hour to the south by rapid train) as we had bought baseball tickets for the Yokohama Baystars vs Nagoya Chunichi Dragons game. Tickets for events are usually available from machines in convenience stores such as Lawson Station or Seven Eleven. But the good seats sell out quite quickly and we had to settle for seats in a rather average part of the stadium instead of the better ones we'd wanted to buy. We took the train to Yokohama Station then did a boat trip around the harbour to the picturesque bayside area where the 'Garden Necklace' festival was in full swing. Basically half the city was decked out with garden displays and flower beds, with accompanying huge crowds and temporary eating establishments.

From the bay it was only a short walk to Yokohama Stadium. We visited the Yokohama team merchandise store just outside the stadium to buy the necessary gear (quite a procedure involving a long queue). We were advised to buy shirts with number 25 on them (Tsutsugo), however 'our man' turned out to be a bit of a disappointment on the day and didn't manage to hit the ball very often. In fact our team didn't get a single home run and the final score was 1–0 to the Dragons. Also, after buying shirts and plastic baseball bats at quite some expense, it turned out to be some sort of 'Girls' Day' celebration, so all women received a free shirt on the way into the stadium. At least it was a different design from the one I had just paid all that money for!

Fortunately the weather was with us, and it actually turned out to be quite hot. The stadium was full to capacity, the baseball game was very fast, the crowd was very lively and loud, the entertainment between innings was fast and furious, and we did a lot of plastic baseball-bat-beating. The man sitting next to us was holding a puppet and both were cheering for the Dragons. The etiquette was straightforward: you only cheer when your team is batting and no-one boos the other team.

Luckily we took our own food, because not only did what was available look unappetising (Kentucky Fried Chicken, hot dogs, hamburgers) but once we were wedged into our seats it would have been difficult to get out to buy anything. Drinks, on the other hand, were plentiful — girls ran up and down the aisles the entire three hours, selling various types of beer and also whiskey with water on tap from backpacks. We didn't see any soft drinks for sale, so it was no wonder the crowd was so vocal given the amount of alcohol being consumed. But as everyone left their seats after the game had finished it was pleasing to see that they took their rubbish with them!

Wedding couple

On Thursday we took a bus tour out of Tokyo to visit two large flower attractions in other prefectures — the Hitachi Seaside Park and the Ashikaga Flower Park. They were both about two hours out of Tokyo, in different directions, and would have taken us forever to reach on our own using public transport.

Both flower parks were spectacular. Hitachi had whole hillsides of blue nemophila flowers (4.5 million plants) and more tulips than you could even imagine (270 types, 260,000 plants). They even provided models dressed as a wedding couple to add interest to visitors' photographs. Delicious lunch bento boxes were available to buy on site at reasonable prices.

Wisteria

Ashikaga had wisteria screens, wisteria trellises, wisteria domes, wisteria tunnels, wisteria arbors, wisteria trees, wisteria pot plants and multitudes of bedding plants, as well as plants for sale (quite cheap compared to Australia). Both flower parks were very popular and crowded, and traffic congestion fairly bad, which made it a 12-hour trip. In between the two flower parks we visited Ichigo no Sato Strawberry Farm, for an all-you-can-eat-in-the-greenhouse organic strawberry picking experience. The strawberries were hands-down the sweetest and most tasty we had ever eaten and many were several mouthfuls in size.

Above: Nemophila at Hitachi Seaside Park

Above: Floral displays at Hitachi Seaside Park; Row Below: Strawberry picking, Ichigo no Sato farm

Romance, Ropeway & Rhododendrons
Hakone: 1–7 May

Above: View of Mount Fuji and Lake Ashi from Onshi-Hakone Koen

Above: Okada Museum of Art, Hakone; Below Left: Sculpture, Hakone Open Air Sculpture Museum; Below Right: Nihonga painting, Narukawa Art Museum

HAKONE: 1–7 May

Romance

After Tokyo we spent a week in the mountain spa town of Hakone, travelling there and back on the special Romance Car train from Shinjuku. It turned out to be Golden Week — a week in which Japanese only need to take a couple of days off work to link several public holidays for a nine-day break. There were huge holiday crowds and the attractions, roads and public transport systems were really congested.

We stayed in a very new K's House Hostel, with its own indoor and outdoor onsens, wonderful views and gorgeous lounge areas. All accommodation was Japanese style with futons on the floor. We were woken up every morning by nightingales singing outside our window.

Ropeway

There is an overwhelming number of attractions in the Hakone area and the 'Hakone 3-day Free Passes' and 'Hakone-Fuji 3-day Free Passes' that we bought ran hot with constant use. The passes covered trains, buses, cable car, ropeway and lake cruises, and also gave discounts to museums and gardens.

The big attraction of the area is of course Mount Fuji, or Fuji-san, which we had visited in 1992. We tried to get there this time by various types of public transport, but it was impossible to get close in a day due to the crowds.

The art museums in the Hakone area are world class, and we visited the five best: the Narukawa Art Museum (with 'Nihonga' art, kaleidoscope collection, and an incredible view of Mount Fuji); the Hakone Open Air Sculpture Museum (chock-a-block with sculptures including a Rodin and many Henry Moores, plus an entire building and two other indoor exhibitions of Picasso works); the Okada Museum of Art (five floors featuring an incredibly valuable collection of Japanese, Chinese and Korean ceramics, screens, and Daum and Galle Art Nouveau glass); the Pola Museum of Art (Picasso and Chagall Dialogue exhibition, permanent exhibition of European masters and outdoor nature and sculpture walk); and the wonderful Lalique Museum.

Rhododendrons

An absolute highlight was the Hakone Botanical Garden of Wetlands, which was so good we visited it twice. Different areas of the Botanical Garden feature deciduous forest, meadow, fen, alpine, marsh and swamp plants. After our second visit we had a lovely lunch at a small restaurant next door and returned home via Lake Ashi. The plants for sale at the Garden were to-die-for, especially the red rhododendrons and red hydrangeas.

Also, in another park on the shores of Lake Ashi, the Onshi-Hakone Koen, there was a lovely display of potted peonies and another marvellous view across the lake to Mount Fuji.

The Hakone area is thermally active. The cable car travels via the sulphurous area of Owakudani, where everyone is issued with protective face cloths. Here you can do a walk and buy black eggs cooked in a thermal hot spring.

One night in Hakone I was woken by an earthquake, though it was just a small tremor. After the two simulations we had done in Fukuoka and in Nara, I immediately recognised what it was. Fortunately it only lasted a few seconds and was so insignificant that Bill managed to sleep through it!

The Key Hiraga Museum, a little-advertised art museum right in the town of Hakone and within walking distance of our accommodation, was interesting. Key Hiraga (1936–2000) was an internationally acclaimed Japanese artist who studied in Paris and produced very colourful pop art using 'a contemporary palette with traditional Japanese techniques' to produce 'provocative exuberant canvases laced with erotic joie de vivre'. Haraga's paintings are displayed in corridors throughout his wife's very old traditional house, which you can wander through after watching a video and having a cup of tea.

After viewing the art we took a train to Odawara where we took time to have lunch, view the castle from its grounds (where there was a community market), wander the streets, visit a temple and walk on the black sandy beach.

Photo Page 129: Owakudani fumaroles, seen from Hakone ropeway

Above & Below Left: Hakone Botanical Garden of Wetlands; Below Right: One of the paintings at the Key Hiraga Museum, Hakone

Birds, Bonsai, & Brakes
Saitama & Tokyo: 8–15 May

CHAPTER THIRTY-TWO

Above & Below: Ushiku Daibutsu

Below: Go-kart, Akihabara

SAITAMA & TOKYO: 8–15 May

Birds

After returning to Tokyo from our week at Hakone, we moved into an Airbnb at Saitama for a few weeks. The apartment was about 20 minutes' walk from Higashi-Urawa Station, just off a main road. In the immediate vicinity along the main roads were several restaurants — soba noodles, Italian, Indian, shabu-shabu (hot-pot) — a sporting goods shop, several supermarkets and drug stores, a Macdonalds (with drive through and home delivery), two clothing shops, a fruit and veg shop, a Seven Eleven, many hairdressers (including the Salon de Koala) and the closest place of all was a 'Cockatiel Farm'!

We visited the 'Papagallo e Topo' Cockatiel Farm one day and had a bit of a chat to the ladies there (who were all wearing pink outfits). They had a large number of differently coloured birds, which all appeared to be very healthy and well cared for. However, after we explained that we were only interested in cockatiels because 1. they were an Australian species, and 2. we owned several back home in Australia, it became clear that because we were travelling around and we plainly wouldn't be buying any birds, they said it was no problem, we could rent one!

The pet business in Japan is huge. There are many dog grooming salons, and even in the summer months it's rare to see dogs being taken for a walk without a coat or other clothing — even trousers are popular. You're likely to see dogs in bicycle baskets and handbags, and many get pushed around town in prams. Most dogs are small, though we saw the occasional large breed. And dogs aren't the only pets to have salons in Japan — the cockatiel shop had an upstairs salon, which, we think, was where you could sit with your rented bird.

Bonsai

There were several local attractions in the Saitama area. We visited the Omiya Bonsai Art Museum, and also the Ushiku Daibutsu, the tallest bronze buddha statue in the world. This enormous buddha is surrounded by fields of flowers, so there was plenty to see in the surrounding grounds. And, unexpectedly, there was also a small children's zoo in the grounds! The buddha statue itself is five storeys high, with plenty of interesting things to see and do inside, in addition to enjoying an excellent view from the top floor.

We did a few excursions into Tokyo during the week, including a day in Akihabara to visit Electric Town, the Kanda Myojin Shrine, the Yushima Seido (Shrine of Confucius) and the very interesting 2k540 crafts district and Chabara food market.

Brakes

I mentioned previously that a train line was closed due to a landslide. Sometimes we had seen 'congestion' listed too, however in Tokyo the usual reason is 'passenger injury'. Line closures for this reason occur almost daily as the suicide rate in Tokyo is quite high and many of the stations don't have guardrails that open and close in conjunction with the train's doors.

Unfortunately we experienced this first hand one day, when the emergency brakes were applied and our train stopped suddenly coming into Ikebukuro Station after a thud. There was an immediate announcement that we didn't understand but a man later told us that passengers were told someone had jumped in front of the train. We could, however, guess what was said from the collective gasp and expressions on people's faces. The announcement had indicated there would be a significant delay and recommended changing to other lines. We were all locked into the carriage for a short while, during which there were further announcements and everyone started texting and making alternative arrangements. It was only a matter of a few more minutes before the doors opened and, when everyone got out, the clean-up squad was already there on the platform. The communications had been timely and efficient.

The next train we took was showing that line 'closed due to passenger injury'. After a day off we were out riding the trains again, but arriving at stations wasn't quite as relaxing as it had been previously.

Photo Page 133: Shabu-shabu restaurant, Saitama

Above & Below Left: Neighbourhood gardens, Saitama; Below Right: Papagallo e Topo Cockatiel farm, Saitama

CHAPTER THIRTY-THREE

Ceremony, Crafts & Crackers
Saitama & Tokyo: 16–23 May

Above Left: Imperial Palace; Below: Saitama Railway Museum, Omiya   Above: Setagaya Tea Ceremony Studio Lempicka, Tokyo

SAITAMA & TOKYO 16–23 May

Ceremony

During the past week we took a tea ceremony lesson and did a tour of the Imperial Palace, both of which were booked over a month before. At the Palace we were part of a group of several hundred, but it was well organised and they catered for many different languages by means of audio guides. We were the only two participants at the tea ceremony lesson, along with an interpreter supplied by the people who hosted our Airbnb. The tea ceremony was a very complex but interesting procedure.

We spent a day in Asakusa at the Sanja Matsuri festival, watching lots of portable shrines being carried in for the following final day of the three-day festival. Sensoji is the oldest temple in Tokyo and the festival is one of Tokyo's most popular, with nearly two million people visiting over the three days of the event.

Crafts

We also visited the Japan Folk Crafts Museum and West Hall near Shibuya in Tokyo. This is a gorgeous small museum displaying beautiful objects from daily life, mainly from the Edo period. We timed our visit to coincide with one of the four days of the month that the West Hall, a well-preserved residence, was open. It was definitely worth visiting.

The main event for the past week was the Grand Sumo Tournament in Tokyo, which is two weeks long and started on 15 May. There are six Grand Sumo Tournaments a year, three of which are held in Tokyo. Tickets were sold out ages before, and we weren't even able to get tickets to watch a training session. However, we managed to be home every day by 3.30 to watch the English TV coverage of the 'maku-uchi' or top-ranked wrestlers fighting it out. Of note are the silk costumes worn by the 'gyoji' (referees), which are to-die-for, with many different outfits being featured each day. Conveniently the matches finish in time for dinner and the six o'clock news.

Three of our Aussie friends arrived on our last Sunday in Saitama to stay with us for a few days. We did the 'must-see' sights with them in Tokyo on two days and spent the other day in the Saitama area. In Tokyo we went to the antiques market in the International Forum building; walked the Marunouchi area; went to the beautiful Palace East Gardens; and visited the Museum of Modern Art and 'animals in craft' exhibition at the Crafts Gallery, Sensoji temple and the luggage museum at Asakusa. We ate lunch at a Yayoiken teishoku restaurant (set meals ordered electronically) then walked along the river to the Ryogoku area and sumo stadium. The visitors were already hooked on sumo by then and we were lucky to get a reasonably good spot amongst the big crowd outside the stadium to catch glimpses of the big name 'rikishi' (wrestlers) rolling up to the stadium in limos. It was very exciting, a bit like royal-watching.

Crackers

One day before our visitors arrived we had a fun time doing a rice cracker-making class in Shinden. On the first day after they arrived we left them at the Edo-Tokyo Museum while we went off to visit the Sumida Hokusai Museum around the corner. This museum is dedicated to the woodblock prints of Katsushika Hokusai (born in the area in 1760), who produced *The Great Wave of Kanagawa*, the most famous of all Japanese woodblocks. Besides the spectacularly beautiful building, the technology of the displays was simply amazing — especially the life-sized models of Hokusai's studio and animatronic figures depicting the artist and his daughter at work — which you would swear blind were real people!

In Saitama we took the visitors to the fabulous Omiya Bonsai Museum and to the Saitama Railway Museum, which had a large display of trains in a very impressive building, as well as some interesting information on the development of the first shinkansen. We had two interesting dinners out, at a local yakitori restaurant and a local shabu-shabu restaurant. We also did a delightful walk around the neighbourhood, with glimpses of suburban life and some incredibly beautiful small gardens, rice fields and veggie plots. Then we travelled to Takayama by bus and three trains.

Photo Page 137: Animatronic figure at Sumida Hokusai Museum, Tokyo

Above: Sanja Festival, Sensoji, Tokyo; Below Left: Sumida Hokusai Museum, Tokyo

Above & Below: Ryogoku Kokugikan Sumo Stadium

Historic district, Hida & Hoba miso
Takayama: 24–30 May

CHAPTER THIRTY-FOUR

141

Above: Taishokoto concert, Jinya, Takayama

Above & Below Left: Shirakawa-go Village; Below Right: Festival floats exhibition hall, Takayama

TAKAYAMA: 24–30 May

Historic district

Our next stop was Takayama, nestled amongst the Japanese Alps. The city has a large, beautifully preserved and fully functioning historic district, called Sanmachi Suji. You can stroll the streets for hours admiring the many temples and shrines, visiting traditional houses, eating at lovely restaurants and visiting sake breweries if inclined.

The morning markets along the river are lively and interesting. Takayama is famous for its 'matsuri' (festivals) in spring and autumn, but at any time of the year you can see a selection of the gorgeous floats (some featuring stages and complicated puppetry) in an exhibition museum in the town.

Another major attraction about an hour out of Takayama is Shirakawa-go, a UNESCO-listed village of thatched-roof houses, which we and our four Australian friends visited on a bus tour. Like Sanmachi Suji, people live and work in the traditional buildings. The buildings have very steeply sloping roofs, thatched with Japanese pampas grass in order to cope with the heavy winter snows. The village is situated in a pretty valley surrounded by mountains that are snow-capped for much of the year.

Hida

One day we spent most of the morning walking around the Hida Folk Village, a really lovely area set amongst natural woodlands and full of traditional buildings, equipment, games and crafts (woodwork, paper-making, pottery, lacquerware, silk-making, weaving and carving).

On the way there we walked up into the hills along back roads and watched rice being planted. On the way home we visited the huge golden roofed Sukyo Mahikari World Shrine. The very elaborate World Shrine, built in 1984, draws on features from many religions — steps based on the Mayan pyramid at Tikal, Islamic minarets, Star of David, Wheel of Dhamma, and a reconstruction of the Quetzalcoatl Fountain in Mexico. It's worth going inside to see the stunning scarlet Great Hall of Worship.

On Sunday we visited the Takayama Jinya, the only old government precinct in Japan to have survived intact — all others having been being burnt down, fallen down or knocked down. It was a large compound where you could visit all the various buildings and rooms, from sleeping quarters to reception rooms, offices, gardens and storerooms. The latter were extensive and filled with interesting museum exhibits — such as the torture room, where 40 kilogram blocks of stone were placed one by one onto a kneeling subject's thighs until they talked. In one of the rooms we were very lucky to hear some beautiful music being played by a group of women on traditional instruments called 'taishokoto'.

Hoba miso

Across the road from the Jinya, there was a weekend-long food festival in one of the long streets in the preservation area of the city. The sake was free to sample and the street food was cheap and delicious. Between six of us we sampled fried whole shrimp, fried octopus, sweet fish (a type of river fish) roasted on skewers, sweet rice balls on skewers, sweet rice crackers, sake and icecreams. Bill had a whole skewered salted 'saba' (mackerel), which he said was delicious.

One night we celebrated three birthdays in our group at a wonderful Japanese restaurant. Amongst other dishes, there was Hida beef and mountain vegetables, which were cooked on individual ceramic charcoal hibachi barbecues, either directly on the grill, or as 'hoba miso,' seasoned with miso (fermented soybean paste) and grilled on magnolia leaves.

A few days later we farewelled our visitors in the morning and spent the day doing chores (going to the post office, buying groceries and getting train tickets) then succumbed to a Japanese Tex-Mex lunch. The next day we re-visited a 100% buckwheat soba noodle restaurant that the group had eaten at earlier, before visiting the Hida Takayama Museum of Art to see their wonderful display of Art Nouveau glass (including Lalique, Galle and Tiffany, among others) and Art Deco furniture. The museum was a welcome relief from the 31°C heat outside.

Photo Page 141: 100% buckwheat soba noodles, Takayama

Above: Weekend food festival, Takayama; Below: Hida Takayama Museum of Art

Soba, Snow wall & Skunk cabbages
Nagano: 31 May–3 June

CHAPTER THIRTY-FIVE

Above: Daizen 100% soba restaurant, Nagano

Above: Ptarmigan merchandise on Alpine Route

Above: Kurobe Cable Car Station; Below: Bus drive between the ice walls

NAGANO: 31 May–3 June

Soba

We stayed in an Airbnb in Nagano, the only city to have hosted events in both winter and summer Olympic Games. The city is ringed by mountains, so we spent a good amount of time exploring them. One day we took a bus up to the Togakushi Shrine area, up past the now snow-less ski fields to the Okusha Shrine. The Shrine is one of three in the area, with a two-kilometre approach path — the first kilometre lined with ferns and other interesting plants, the second kilometre lined with majestic cedar trees. On the way back, we turned off at the halfway point gate and returned via the second shrine on a path that took us for several kilometres through the Togakushi Forest Botanical Garden and through a forest and around two lovely lakes. There were serious-looking signs warning about bear activity but we didn't encounter any.

Further down the mountain we visited the Soba Museum, where according to the literature they run lessons in making soba noodles. It could only happen in Japan — we walked in, there were no other visitors around, and a minute later we were having a personal noodle-making lesson. We left with the noodles we'd made, as well as a buckwheat icecream each for the bus ride home.

Snow wall

On another day we completed the Tateyama Kurobe Alpine Route, a trip across the Japanese Alps by a variety of transport: 1. bus from home to Nagano Station, 2. express bus to Ogizawa, 3. tunnel trolley bus, 4. cable car, 5. ropeway, 6. another tunnel trolley bus, 7. highland bus, 8. cable car, 9. express train to Toyama, 10. shinkansen back to Nagano, and 11. bus from Nagano station to home.

While there are a number of attractions along the Alpine Route (views, dam, waterfalls, lakes, wetland flowers, forests), the highlight of the trip is supposed to be a walk along the 'Uki-no-Otani' or Snow Wall, a kilometre of roadway lying between walls of snow that start out being around 19 metres tall when the walkway opens in mid-April, but which become increasingly shorter towards August. Unfortunately we had to forgo all the attractions and make do with viewing the ice walls from a bus because walking was cancelled on the day due to blizzard conditions with -1°C temperature, hard snow and near-whiteout at all viewing spots!

We had heard a lot about the Alpine Route, but found it difficult to reach in a day trip from the other places we'd stayed at. It seems to be most popular as an overnight excursion from one of the major cities. Nevertheless, we managed to do it in a single long day, and it was definitely worth it. It was quite an experience, even though we had to imagine what we missed from the stunning photos on display.

Skunk cabbages

The main attraction in Nagano city itself is the Zenkoji Temple, which we visited one morning before having a lovely hot soba and vegetable lunch at Daizen, a restaurant in town at which all the soba noodles are made from 100% buckwheat. Like many popular restaurants in Japan, we had to add our details to a list at the door then wait on a bench outside until a table became available.

During our stay the skunk cabbages were in bloom in wetland areas, along with many other wildflowers. Rice had just been planted in the now flooded fields — here in the mountains surrounding Nagano, there is only a single crop each year. The climate is ideal for growing buckwheat, which would have been planted in early May.

Our Airbnb in Nagano didn't have clothes-washing facilities, so we did our washing at the laundromat across the road before leaving. As you'd expect, laundromat facilities are pretty good in Japan. There are all sorts of washing and drying machines (including ones for sneakers), and they also have a variety of sizes and combinations of washer/driers. You just put the washing in and the machine adds detergent, washes and dries the clothes in a single operation, so you know exactly what time to return and collect your washing. Naturally there are seats, trolleys and sorting tables.

Photo Page 145: Making soba noodles, Tonkururen Togakushi Soba Museum

Above: Zuiji-mon Gate, on walk to Okusha Shrine

Above: Kagami-Ike Pond; Below Left: Skunk cabbage; Below Right: Making soba noodles, Tonkururen Togakushi Soba Museum

Kites, Kamo aquarium & Kitchen equipment
Niigata & Tsuruoka: 4–11 June

149

Above & Below: Kite festival, Nakanokuchi River, Shirone

Above: Niigata Manga Animation Museum

NIIGATA & TSURUOKA: 4–11 June

Kites

We left Nagano and travelled north by train to spend four nights in Niigata. On our first day there we visited the Media Ship Building in Niigata, where you can get 20-storey views for free, as well as enjoying a really lovely and interesting garden on the fourth floor.

In the afternoon we were fortunate enough to catch the final day of the five-day annual battle of the giant kites at Shirone, about an hour by bus out of Niigata. Two opposing teams at a time battle across the Nakanokuchi River using giant kites. The teams are made up of residents, who spend all year making and painting huge numbers of kites of various sizes up to seven x three metres.

Each team lines up on their side of the river and groups of up to 25 people run the kites into flight. The airborne kites become tangled, plummet into the river and the teams engage in a cross-river tug-o'-war until the ropes break. The winning team has the greater total amount of opponents' rope pulled over to their side. The huge kites can be quite dangerous when they plummet into the crowd, as we were told when we inadvertently wandered into the danger zone.

On the way home we dropped into the Sake Museum at Niigata Station to learn a bit more about the sake-making process and to enjoy some sake tasting. There were 111 different types of sake and you could taste any five at a time for 500 yen. It seemed like a good place for people to drop in for a drink after hopping off the train, and was a great way of comparing types and brands of sake before purchasing a bottle to take home.

The following day we visited the Fukushimagata Wetland, with its huge number of species of native birds and plants, a wonderful indoor educational display and observation deck with plenty of telescopes.

Courtesy of a lift to the local station with the director of the Wetland Museum who took pity on us when he found out we had walked the last 2.5 kilometres to reach the place, we headed back to town for a personalised evening tour of the Imayo Tsukasa Sake Brewery that we had booked the day before. For 500 yen (300 actually, because we had a discount voucher), we could taste up to 17 different types of sake.

On our last day in Niigata we used the city-loop bus to visit Hakusan Koen Park and shrine, some lovely old houses, the fish market (for lunch), and the Niigata Manga Animation Museum (interesting and fun).

Kamo aquarium

After Niigata we travelled to Tsuruoka and the following day took a bus to the start of the Mount Haguro pilgrimage walk, a 1.7 kilometre climb up 2446 steps on a stone path lined with cedars amidst beautiful forest, with many smaller shrines along the way and a 'Mirror Lake' full of green frogs at the top. The summit can also be reached by bus so we walked up but caught the bus back to the station.

The Kamo Jellyfish Aquarium is certainly worth a visit while you're in Tsuruoka. There wasn't a penguin or dolphin in sight, but it had the world's greatest collection of jellyfish and comb jellies. The display was incredible, and there was a fabulous laboratory for learning about the aquarium's highly successful jellyfish-breeding techniques.

Kitchen equipment

The information counter at Tsuruoka station 'rents' out bicycles for free, so on another day we obtained bikes and rode to Tsuruoka Park for lunch before visiting the Chido Museum, a very interesting place chock-a-block with interesting craft works, kitchen equipment and fishing and farm implements, as well as ancient boats, tools and ceramics.

Next morning there was heavy rain, thunder, lightning and hail, so we didn't venture out until the afternoon — when we did a long walk around the city with visits to the Chidokan Clan School (an 1805 educational establishment) and the Tsuruoka Art Forum (a modern building for creative groups to make and display artworks). But it was the new city Cultural Centre under construction next door — designed by Kazuyo Sejima — that took our breath away.

Photo Page 149: Kitchen equipment, Chido Museum, Tsuruoka

Above: Tsuruoka Cultural Centre under construction

Above: Kamo Jellyfish Aquarium; Below: Sake Museum tasting, Niigata Station

Above: Mount Haguro walk

Tsuguharu, Turning dolls & Tanbo art
Akita, Hirosaki & Kuroishi: 12–15 June

Above: Suikinkutsu water cave, Fujita Garden, Hirosaki; Below Left: Big Kokeshi doll, Kuroishi; Below Right: Neputa Festival lantern

Below: Shamisen musicians

AKITA, HIROSAKI & KUROISHI: 12–15 June

Tsuguharu

We stopped off at Akita on our way to Kuroishi, to break the all-day trip on local trains. Akita is the home of akita dogs, the very handsome ones with curled up tails that seem to be one of the most common breeds in Japan.

Our purpose was to visit the Akita Museum of Art, designed by Ando Tadao in 2015. Photos weren't allowed inside, but it was spectacular, with a freestanding spiral staircase, a huge triangular skylight, and a cafe with edge-pool view looking over to the former museum building and lotus pond across the road. Both old and new museums were designed to feature a 20 x 3.6 metre mural called 'Annual Events in Akita' — a captivating, colourful and lively painting by Fujita Tsuguharu completed in 1937.

We thought we were in for a restful few days in Kuroishi as it is a small town in a very rural area specialising in apple and rice growing. The highlights of the town were proclaimed to be old samurai residences and sake breweries, both of which we had seen plenty of already. But, like elsewhere, we found there were many unexpected things to see and do.

We spent a day in the 'big smoke' of Hirosaki, about half an hour away by train. The Fujita Memorial Garden was outstanding, not the least because it featured a suikinkutsu (also called a 'water harp' or 'water cave') that was loud enough to be heard without the need of its bamboo pipe. The suikinkutsu has an underground ceramic chamber with water slowly dripping into it; the sound is amplified by the chamber and usually can only be heard with your ear to the pipe.

The Hirosaki Castle Botanical Garden was also full of interest, including a very comprehensive display of roses, a wetland, and many displays of hedging plants and topiary. Our combined ticket included Hirosaki Castle, otherwise we wouldn't have gone there (we had seen about twelve castles so far). However this one turned out to be particularly interesting because they were repairing the wall it had sat upon (each rock was numbered) and in order to do this the castle had been moved 70 metres from its original place to a new location. Excellent interpretation was provided on the mechanics of the move, with a video and various signs and pieces of machinery on display. The move involved rails and turntables, and the procedure was completed in 70 days — not a bad timeframe for moving a castle!

Turning dolls

We also visited the Arts and Handcrafts Centre in Hirosaki, where we watched a performance of shamisen (Japanese guitars) and taiko (Bill was invited to play one of the drums) and saw all the various local handcrafts in action (indigo-dyed cloth, kokeshi dolls, lacquerware, paper lanterns) as well as a display of the huge Neputa lanterns that are used in the street parades of the annual Neputa festival in August.

The following day our Airbnb host arranged for us to have a two-hour hands-on lesson painting kokeshi dolls, which was accomplished by turning the dolls on a small lathe. It was a really fun experience thanks to our expert teacher Kon Kaneo. We purchased one of Kon's exquisite kokeshi doll chess sets.

Tanbo-art

In the afternoon we hired bicycles from the visitor information centre at Kuroishi station and rode out to a small town a couple of kilometres away called Tanbo-Art. Every year the townspeople plant several rice paddies in designs selected by competition and the special station opens for visitors to access the art by train.

We had seen the surveyors on site from the train the day we arrived, and a couple of days later, from the purpose-built tower, we watched the rice planters in action and could almost make out what the final picture would look like in a few weeks' time (samurai, akita dogs and text). Designs in the past have included Mount Fuji, Star Wars and the Mona Lisa, to name only a few. For the rest of the year, when the rice fields are empty, there are two permanent pictures made of rocks in the car park areas, featuring Princess Diana and Yujiro Ishihara, a famous Japanese actor/poet.

Photo Page 153: Neputa festival lantern, Arts and Handcraft Centre, Hirosaki

Above: Art in carpark — actor/poet Yujiro Ishiharav

Above: Completed Kokeshi dolls; Below: Planting field for Tanbo-Art (rice paddy art)

Above: Painting Kokeshi dolls, Kuroishi

Bicycles, Best film & Big bath
Tazawako & Yamagata: 16–23 June

Above: Bicycling around Lake Tazawako

Above: Statue of Tatsuko; Below: Lake Tazawako

Above: Beech forest, Nyuto

TAZAWAKO & YAMAGATA: 16–23 June

Bicycles

We spent four nights at beautiful Lake Tazawako in the 'That Sounds Good Jazz Pension' — which was relaxing in an energetic sort of way. The pension supplied bicycles so we spent our first full day bicycling twenty kilometres around the lake. The next day we walked into town (about nine kilometres) to buy rail tickets, passing through villages and alongside crop fields (mainly rice and buckwheat) and vegetable gardens. We walked a further few kilometres back to our accommodation via a lovely herb/garden centre. It was a very beautiful part of the world and the weather was perfect.

On our last full day at Lake Tazawako we took a bus to Nyuto Onsen in the nearby mountains and spent a couple of hours walking downhill taking photos, partly along the road (where there were hundreds of different insects on the plants), but mostly on woodchip paths through a beautiful beech forest. We stopped at every plant and insect along the way, then caught the bus back, had a dip in the very cold lake before relaxing in our onsen at the pension. During the entire stay our host cooked us wonderful breakfasts and dinners using all sorts of local vegetables and herbs along with chicken and seafood. The food was excellent, the setting superb, and the music was great despite no live shows.

For lunches we bought skewered chicken and miso-covered pounded rice cakes on two days at a service centre further along the lake, and on the other day we ate at the nearby Tazawako Heart Herb Garden. The Heart Herb Centre had a comprehensive range of plants for sale, as well as an outdoor herb garden.

From Tazawako we moved south to Yamagata, where we stayed for four nights at a hotel conveniently close to the station. Yamagata is in the mountainous region of northern Japan, and the city itself is surrounded by ski fields up to around 1700 metres elevation. We tried to visit the Okama Crater Lake, but the weather was against us. With strong winds, rain and total whiteout at the top of the mountain, the bus was cancelled.

Best film

With the bus to the top of the mountain cancelled, we left the city and visited Kaminoyama (with another castle, a very nice footbath, and the location of the film set for 'Departures' — the first Japanese movie to win an Oscar for Best Foreign Film), then returned to Yamagata and visited the castle (two castles in one day had to be a record!) and also the Yamagata Museum of Art.

The latter opened in 1964 and was the first regional art gallery in Japan to start collecting modern paintings, by artists including Monet, Van Gogh, Cezanne, Matisse, Degas, Chagall and Picasso, as well as important Japanese paintings, sculptures and calligraphy. This was a lovely way to spend the rest of a wet day.

We tried again for the crater lake in the mountains the following day, but the bus only went halfway up the mountain, where we spent a couple of hours in the mist looking at alpine plants on a rather bleak ski field.

Big bath

Fortunately, on our last full day in Yamagata, the weather cleared enough for a visit to Zao Onsen. From there we took numerous ropeways and chairlifts and had a wonderful day walking around ski slopes, through forests, and to mountain ponds. The top of the mountain was around 1750 metres and quite cool at 11°C, whereas the city below was sweltering in 28°C heat.

At the end of the day we hiked up a steep clearing covered with white daisies on the ski slope beneath the Zao sky cable to visit a very blue and sulphurous outdoor onsen (the Zao Onsen Dai-Roten-Buro or big open-air bath) located in a small ravine that had a river running through it, before heading back to Zao Onsen and catching the bus back to Yamagata.

This time of the year the cherries are delicious, though quite expensive (because they are perfect). We decided not to visit any of the many cherry-picking orchards because they weren't accessible by train alone, and the additional taxi fares would have made the whole exercise rather too expensive.

Photo Page 157: Zao Onsen big open air bath Dai Roten Buro

Above: View from Mount Sanpokojin

Above: Nature walk from cable car; Below: Daisies under Zao Sky Cable   Above: Flowers Juhyo Kogent

Samurai, Soymilk skin & Shiki-shima
Nikko & Tokyo: 24–28 June

CHAPTER THIRTY-NINE

Above: Nikko Railway Station designed by Frank Lloyd Wright

Above: Newly planted edamame; Below: Boardwalk through Senjogahara Moor

NIKKO & TOKYO: 24–28 June

Samurai

Nikko was fabulous. At only 150 km from Tokyo, its history and natural landscape make it a mecca for tourists and school groups. We stayed for four nights at the Nikko Suginamiki Youth Hostel, a rather remote place 2.3 kilometres from the nearest rural train station — Shimotsuke-Osawa station on the JR Nikko Line. But what a find! We phoned from the station and the host picked us up. We booked in for breakfasts and dinners — both of which were not only cheap but also substantial, and featured local specialties and ingredients cooked with gluten-free ingredients and with chicken substituted for pork, specially for us.

On the Saturday night there were other guests, but it was just us for the rest of the time. The place was large and rambling with lovely Japanese-style tatami rooms and large shared baths, and was run by a very lovely family who spoke excellent English. The place also featured a large hall, where regular group activities were held. On the first night we were invited to watch the 25-strong ken-do class — samurai training — which was incredibly interesting. On the day we left we were presented with our very own 'tenugui' or ken-do headscarves.

Soymilk skin

Our hosts drove us to the station each morning, but we walked home in the evenings — past houses, gardens and through farmland and forests. We were almost able to watch the rice growing! And with the help of the hosts, we learned what many of the other crops were. The edamame (soybeans), which had been planted just before we arrived, were about 20 centimetres tall by the end of our stay. We had some of last year's crop served hot with garlic and butter as part of our dinner one night. They also cooked us one of the local dishes, 'yuba', or soymilk skin.

The World Heritage Toshogu Shrine complex at Nikko is very extensive, and features the most ornately ornamented of all the temples in Japan. We visited on a Sunday but the queue for the main temple was so long that we opted for a five-kilometre forest walk instead, then returned to see the temple on a weekday. Interestingly one of the temples was being renovated, and a whole four- or five-storey building had been built around it to shield the construction work.

Along the two-kilometre walk up to the temple area from Nikko JR Station (designed by Frank Lloyd Wright) there's a myriad of souvenir shops and restaurants, and we found a really interesting potato cafe that served cold cooked sweet potatoes with yoghurt and coffee. Might sound unusual, but we went there twice it was so good. About half way to the temple area is an excellent information centre, with far more information than you will get from the counter at the station.

Shiki-shima

On the day with the best weather (it was the rainy season!) we took a bus into the mountains for a four-hour walk via two beautiful waterfalls, through the Senjogahara Moor, and around Lake Yunoko, with just enough time at the end at Yumoto Onsen to enjoy the free outdoor footbath (but not for long, the water was so hot) before catching a return bus to Nikko station.

Parked at Nikko station was the 'Shiki-shima', the Japanese luxury train that costs between $3,000 and $10,000 per night (you have to apply by ballot and it's booked out way ahead). It does various two-day to four-day trips to tourist destinations around Japan and has its own platform — number 13½ at Ueno Station in Tokyo.

After our weekday visit to the temple complex we spent the rest of that day at the Nikko Botanical Garden, a research garden of Tokyo University. We were told that the route around the Garden would probably take an hour, but we ended up spending three hours as there were so many unusual plants, so many insects, and such beautiful ponds and wetlands — full of forget-me-nots and frogs. And not a gaijin (foreigner) in sight!

From Nikko we returned to Tokyo for one night at the Super Lohas Hotel (with lovely onsen) before heading to Hokkaido on the shinkansen.

Photo Page 161: Ema (wooden votive plaques) at Kannon-do Shrine, Nikko

Above & Row Below: Toshogu Shrine, Nikko

CHAPTER FORTY

Picking cherries, Polar bears & Poppies
Sapporo, Asahikawa & Daisetsuzan: 29 June–3 July

Above: Kaneto Ainu Museum, Asahikawa　　Above: Grids Hotel and Hostel, Susukino, Sapporo

Above: Seal display, Asahiyama Zoo; Below: Penguin display, Asahiyama Zoo

SAPPORO, ASAHIKAWA & DAISETSUZAN: 29 June–3 July

Picking cherries

Our journey from Tokyo was exciting — we had splurged and bought Gran Class tickets on the Hayabusa 13 shinkansen from Tokyo to Shin-Hakodate Hokuto in Hokkaido, a 4¼-hour trip travelling half the length of Japan at between 260 and 320 km/hr. After that, the 300 kilometre train trip on the Super Hakuto Limited Express from Shin-Hakodate to Sapporo took nearly as long.

After arriving in Hokkaido, the northernmost of the main Japanese islands, we stayed for two nights in Susukino, the entertainment area of Sapporo, at Grids Hotel and Hostel. It was a relatively new and very friendly place. Although the staff organised an okonomiyaki cooking night, we opted to go out on the town for dinner, and ended up at a very nice Spanish tapas bar.

We spent the following day in Sapporo doing catchup things such as haircuts (around $12 at the QB House walk-ins which are all around Japan), washing and shopping. The next day we picked up a hire car near Sapporo Station to drive around Hokkaido for the next month. We had taken advantage of a great monthly half-price deal on car hire. After travelling around Hokkaido we would be spending August back in a suburb of Sapporo, with various groups of friends visiting during our last month in Japan.

From Sapporo we drove to Asahikawa, in the centre of Hokkaido. We drove north out of the city along the coast road and were lucky enough to find an all-you-could-eat-cherry-picking orchard for lunch (the cherries were delicious!) before turning inland to the 'Green House', our Airbnb in Asahikawa.

Polar bears

On the first day in Asahikawa we went to the local zoo (Asahiyama), which specialises in Hokkaido and cold-climate animals, such as polar bears, penguins, seals, arctic foxes, brown bears and hares. It's the only zoo we've come across with a tunnel for viewing penguins swimming, and there was a special 'room' with nesting penguins tending their eggs. The zoo had a multitude of hand-made signs and cutouts, and although not terribly professional-looking, the cutouts were very effective for demonstrating relative sizes of animals. Another nice touch was a number of 'bubbles' that you could climb up into from below for a 'seal's eye view' of the polar bears — including one with a periscope for wheelchair-bound visitors. We also visited the Ainu (aboriginal people) museum, which was interesting, though it was sad learning about the persecution and subsequent fight to keep their culture alive.

Poppies

We did a day trip from Asahikawa to Daisetsuzan, Japan's largest national park. From the very informative visitor centre at Sounkyo Onsen we took a ropeway up to a lovely garden of alpine plants. There was so much mist that we didn't bother to take the chairlift up further, besides which the walk to the top of Mount Kurodake was still closed due to snow. Back at the bottom, we did an hour-long walk up to Momojidani waterfall, keeping our voices raised to ward off the bears we were assured were lurking in the forest. We saw two more waterfalls in the main part of Sounkyo Gorge, but the main feature was the columnar rock formation. It was 20°C that day, compared to the -20°C we experienced in the middle of winter when we visited in 1992. Being at 20°C was more comfortable than being in other parts of Japan, which were sweltering in the mid-30s, with a typhoon bringing torrential rain and flooding in Kyushu. On the way home we visited the beautiful Daisetsu Mori no Garden, with gorgeous displays of all sorts of flowering plants, including three species of blue poppies, two of which were in flower.

From Asahikawa we completed the longest drive we would do in Hokkaido, to Wakkanai. While the distances weren't great (the trip was under 300 kilometres), the speed limit is so low that it seems to take ages to get anywhere. The general limit when unmarked is 60 km/hr, but in marked areas it's 40 or 50 km/hr. Only on a few expressways and toll roads can you do 70 or 80 km/hr. On the open road, drivers generally don't seem to travel more than 10 km/hr over the speed limit.

Photo Page 165: Fur cushions, Kaneto Ainu Museum, Asahikawa

Above: Walk to Momojidani waterfall; Below: Woodpecker holes

Above: Blue poppy, Daisetsu Mori no Garden; Below: Flowers, Mount Kurodake

Black-haired beef, Boats & Boardwalk
Wakkanai & Rebun Island: 4–10 July

Above: Fishing nets on coast, Wakkanai; Below: Barn, Milk Road, Wakkanai

WAKKANAI & REBUN ISLAND: 4–10 July

Black-haired beef

Wakkanai is the northernmost town in Japan, with street signs in both Japanese and Russian, and where you can get a ferry across to the Russian Sakhalin Island (5½ hours). In winter Wakkanai hosts a dog sleigh contest on the airport runway and the sea freezes over.

In a week we did most of the sightseeing available — Cape Soya and Cape Noshappu (both with an extraordinary number of monuments and statues), the arched breakwater dome and colonnade at the ferry port, Wakkanai Station (northernmost in Japan), the Wakkanai Aquarium and adjoining Science Museum (neither really worth the visit), the fishing port, Meguma Marsh and boardwalk, Onuma Bird House and lake (famous for migrating white swans but none at the time), the Mega Solar Plant, the Soya Hills (cattle and wind farms), and the Milk Road (it's a huge dairy and black-haired beef area). We travelled mainly by car, with not a lot of walking because of strong winds, fog and occasional rain.

Our accommodation was the lovely yellow Pension Arumeria about 15 kilometres out of Wakkanai, right on the beach in the middle of nowhere, with its own onsens. Apart from the fact that you can see seals, white-tailed eagles (and Steller's sea eagles in winter) and, supposedly on a clear day, Sakhalin Island, the food there was simply amazing — especially the seafood.

We thought we'd come across most foods in Japan already, but here we were served the most exquisite array of seafoods — including pickled sea cucumber, octopus shabu-shabu, octopus head, octopus gills, three types of clams, three types of prawns, whelks, squid, sea urchin roe, salmon roe, king crab, hairy crab, two types of scallops, and some very unusual fish such as flying fish and karei (right eyed flounder) which had a jelly-like consistency. Many of the vegetables were a bit slimy but good, such as okra, daikon, mushrooms and seaweeds.

We were somewhat unlucky with the weather in Wakkanai as it remained foggy and windy for the whole week, with a bit of rain thrown in. But it was still refreshing to be somewhere a bit wild, and to see some of the wildlife, including quite a few foxes.

Boats

We took the two-hour ferry on the best day (of a bad bunch) over to Rebun Island, one of the two offshore islands that belong to the Sarobetsu National Park (the other being Rishiri). There we did the eight-kilometre forest walk that went via a field of endemic eidelweiss. The eidelweiss were growing with other wildflowers on a steep slope that we thought went down to the ocean, though it was hard to tell in the mist. On the ferry ride over to the island we met and chatted to the ship's engineer. We were sitting on regular seats, whereas in the boat on the way back we sat, and at times lay down, in 'Japanese style' raised floor areas. After our walk it was quite pleasant to have a two-hour nap on the trip back to Wakkanai. Most people either lay down and slept or watched TV.

Boardwalk

We had visited two coastal wetland areas on the way to Wakkanai from Asahikawa — Sarobetsu and Horonobe — both of which had fine visitor centres. The latter wetland was more extensive, so one day we returned to do a six-kilometre walk, most of which was along a boardwalk.

Although it was mostly foggy or rainy during our week in Wakkanai, we were lucky in a way because at least it was cool to cold the whole time, while the rest of Japan and other parts of Hokkaido were experiencing temperatures in the mid 30s. We took the coast road out of Wakkanai to our next stop at Monbetsu, and along the way (also from Monbetsu to Abashiri) there were many lakes and 'primitive plant gardens', with associated car camping, food, souvenirs and toilets.

It was lovely driving around this part of Hokkaido, with its beautiful coloured barns, cattle, lush green grass, and extensive open landscape dotted with wind farms. With the amount of fog, it wasn't hard to imagine the countryside covered in snow in winter.

Photo Page 169: Miso soup with Hokkaido baby scallops, Pension Arumeria

Above: View from Sarabetsu Wetland to Mount Rishiri on Rishiri Island

Above: Tower of Prayer for Korean Airlines flight KAL007, Cape Soya

Above: Endemic Eidelweiss, Rebun Island Forest Course walk; Below: Rebun port

Shells, Sea angels & Sea ice
Monbetsu & Abashiri: 11–16 June 2017

Above: Big snow crab claw, Monbetsu

Above: Sea angel (Clione); Below: Tokoro Curling Centre

MONBETSU & ABASHIRI: 11–16 July

Sea angels

After driving down the eastern coast road of Hokkado from Wakkanai, we spent two nights in Monbetsu, where the main feature of interest was the Okhotsk Sea Ice Museum. Here you could experience the -20°C ice room, blow frozen bubbles, and view local plants and animals beautifully displayed in blocks of ice.

Monbetsu and Abashiri are on the Sea of Okhotsk, and in winter they experience the lowest latitude sea ice of anywhere. Icebreaker trips feature as winter attractions. There's an underwater observatory in Monbetsu for viewing the marine life under the sea ice in winter — in particular 'sea angels' (pteropods, which are tiny planktonic animals).

We saw most of the other attractions in Monbetsu — including a seal rehabilitation facility, an observatory, a lovely park built in a disused quarry, an historic village, and a stunning flower garden. On the way to Abashiri we took a serendipitous wrong turn and came across the Tokoro Curling Centre, where we spent a good hour or so watching some of the best teams from all over Japan playing. Though it's played on ice, curling seems to be the closest game in Japan to our Australian lawn bowls.

Sumo

We only had to suffer two hot days (out of the ten days of a current heatwave) after arriving in Abashiri. We spent most of one day in the air-conditioned comfort of Kitami Hospital, while I had an eye problem checked out. While waiting, we saw high school students being brought in with heat exhaustion. The eye problem turned out not to be serious and would mend by itself — I was told it was just due to old age! We found the Japanese health system to be excellent — efficient, thorough and cheap by Australian standards.

The road to Kitami took us inland through a stunning farming landscape. The many colourful barns with peaked or curved roofs, housing cattle and hay, were simply gorgeous. We also noticed many strange fences along the country roads in this part of Hokkaido, which we believed to be snow fences with aerofoils to direct blowing snow so that it wouldn't accumulate on the road in winter.

The other hot day was 36°C so we visited the (largely) outdoor Abashiri Prison Museum first thing in the cool of the morning, before heading to the Museum of Northern Peoples and the Okhotsk Ryu-hyo Museum, both of which were nicely air-conditioned. All three attractions had state-of-the-art displays and catered for English-speaking visitors in different ways. Abashiri Prison has a chilling reputation, with inmates put to work in harsh conditions to build a road across central Hokkaido. Both the history and the architectural features of the prison were fascinating.

We generally arrived back home to air conditioned accommodation by about four o'clock, but this week we had the extra incentive of the live TV coverage of the Grand Sumo Tournament in Nagoya, with English commentary between four and six o'clock.

Shells

We spent our last day in Abashiri driving around country roads through huge stretches of farmland with wheat, barley, corn, potatoes, onions, asparagus and daikon. As well, we drove along the coast road to the Tofutsu Lake Bird Observatory (visited by thousands of whooper swans in winter) and the Koshimizu Natural Flower Garden, an area with huge numbers of yellow lillies and purple irises in bloom, along with many other wildflowers.

Back in town we went to the excellent Moyoro Shell Mound Museum, whose exhibits showcase the way of life of the 1300-year-old Moyoro people who venerated bears and were skilled at hunting marine mammals.

On the day we left Abashiri we called in to visit two artists (a botanical artist and her lithographer husband) with whom we had stayed for several days in winter in 1992. It was wonderful to find that they still lived in the same lovely house in the forest overlooking Lake Abashiri — which had been frozen and sprinkled with ice fishing holes on our visit in 1992.

Above: Bear skulls, Moyoro Shell Mound Museum; Below: Koshimizu Park

Brown bears, Binoculars & Buoys
Rausu & Shiretoko: 17–20 July

Above: Mount Rausu from Shiretoko Pass road; Below: Two brown bears spotted from boardwalk

RAUSU & SHIRETOKO: 17–20 July

Brown bears

We spent most of the week at Rausu, a fishing town with easy access to Shiretoko National Park. Shiretoko is World Heritage listed and is perhaps the most unspoilt area of Japan. Human visitation seems to be managed very well in this national park, with several large interpretive centres for visitors pushing the concept that people are 'visiting the brown bears in their homes'. Most of the peninsula is inaccessible except to experienced trekkers, and landing from boats is forbidden.

Our hotel near Rausu was a relatively expensive one, but worth it for the excellent meals and its own indoor and outdoor onsens. There was also a geyser just up the road next to a visitor centre. The geyser erupted roughly every hour. On weekends the staff at the visitor centre kept a record of eruption times so the next eruption would be roughly predictable. But they didn't do this on weekdays — I must have just missed an eruption and waited nearly an hour for the next one. The area was rife with black flies (like our sandflies) and I accumulated 36 bites over that time.

This time of year is the 'active bear season' in Shiretoko, so the only way we were allowed do the beautiful Goko Lakes three-hour ground walk (there is an 800 metre-long raised boardwalk with electric fence that is permanently open) was to book on a guided walk that included bear-encounter training.

When we arrived at the visitor centre, we found that our walk had been cancelled due to bear activity along the track. However, we waited around until the track re-opened and managed to get on a later walk with an excellent guide who pointed out many interesting features along the way — including bear claw marks on trees, woodpecker holes in trees, and fresh bear droppings.

On the way back on the boardwalk our guide spotted two adult brown bears munching their way through the grass on a nearby hill. It was wonderful to see, from a safe distance, these large and dangerous animals in the wild. Fortunately I had remembered just in time (during the bear training session) to offload the snack bars from my pack!

Binoculars

Although we got a glimpse of the spectacular Mount Rausu emerging from the clouds on the drive in, both the Shiretoko Pass and Rausu town were in fog for virtually the entire time we were staying there. On the second day we did a three-hour walk to Lake Rausu, which was very atmospheric, with bright orange cow lillies standing out vividly in the fog.

We had intended to do a whale-watching trip on the last day, but, because of the fog, we drove up the coast instead to visit the Rusa Field House and see two interesting free onsens (one at the low tide mark, the other enclosed in sheds). We were able to use the telescopes and binoculars at the field house but, although there were supposed to be sperm whales and orcas around at the time, there weren't any to be seen. We were very fortunate, however, to find that it was konbu (seaweed) harvesting time.

There was a konbu display in the Field House and along the coast we saw fishermen in small boats collecting the huge kelp fronds from the offshore farms, processing them on the beaches, and hanging them out to dry in sheds. Afterwards, back in town, we visited an interesting photographic exhibition about the early days of kelp harvesting in the Rausu area.

Buoys

After leaving Rausu for Teshikaga we visited the Shibetsu Salmon Museum and the Notsuke Peninsula where there were even more irises in flower than we'd seen previously, and where we were lucky enough to spot two wild red-crowned cranes in the salt marsh.

The entire coastline in this part of Japan is set with huge fixed fishing nets, marked by coloured buoys extending way out to sea. It's also a huge salmon producing area (fingerlings are raised here and released to return as adults four years later) and sea urchin and scallop fishing are also important.

Photo Page 177: Tree with brown bear scratch marks, Shiretoko National Park

Row Above: Konbu (kelp) processing after harvesting, Rausu coast; Below: Tree, Lake Rausu walk; Below Right: Cow lillies, Lake Rausu walk

Marimo, Mining & MOO
Teshikaga & Kushiro: 21–26 July

Above: Onneto hot waterfall

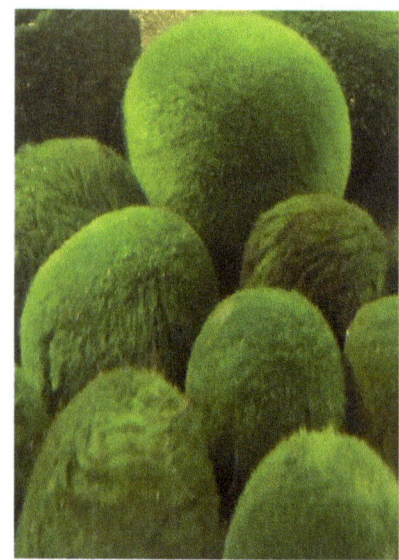
Above: Marimo algae balls, Lake Akan

Above: Plants near Lake Mashu; Below: Kelp drying on gravel, Kiritappu coast

TESHIKAGA & KUSHIRO: 21–26 July

Marimo

We stayed in Teshikaga for three nights. From there it was quite easy to get to Akan National Park. Every day was foggy (actually most days in Hokkaido had been!) but we ventured out into the countryside anyway and some days the fog lifted for short spells.

We visited Lake Onneto which was shrouded in fog. However, it fined up a bit for a walk to the Onneto Hot Waterfall. This, we believe, is the only place in the world where manganese is precipitated from hot spring water by a microbial process. After walking to the waterfall we took a cruise on Lake Akan to see where giant green spheres of algae (called 'marimo') form under just the right conditions of water movement.

While in the area, we also visited the interesting Taiho Koki Sumo Museum (Taiho was a famous Sumo wrestler from Hokkaido), as well as doing a short nature walk around the Wakoto Peninsula at Lake Kussharo. The latter area seems to be popular with kayakers and standup paddle-boarders, and there was even a group yoga class on boards. The lake water seemed quite warm and there was a beach where you could dig out your own onsen in the sand.

Mining

We spent another day in Akan National Park before the arrival of some torrential rain. The panoramic views of the two crater lakes, Lake Mashu and Lake Kussharo, eluded us until the fog lifted briefly on the way home. Meanwhile we visited Mount Iwo, a spectacularly bare mountain, with active fumaroles, that used to be mined for sulphur.

After Teshikaga, we stayed in Kushiro for three nights at the lovely Guest House Yasumizaka. There the hosts run a curry restaurant at lunchtime (while the staying guests are out and about) and they kindly let us order curries in the morning to have for our dinner (one keema curry, one Thai style chicken soup curry, both with a Japanese twist and both delicious).

We spent another day exploring the coast to the east of Kushiro as far as Hamanaka and the aptly named Cape Kiritappu ('kiri' meaning fog), where we were lucky to observe the next stages of konbu (kelp) processing. The fronds, which had been laid out on gravel to absorb the mist (yes, another foggy day!), were being bundled up and loaded onto trucks. One of the workers presented us with a bundle of soft konbu, which our guest house host steamed with vegetables to include with our breakfast the following day.

MOO

Our other day in Kushiro was spent visiting various red-crowned crane centres in the Kushiro-Shitsugen National Park. The long boardwalk through the swamp from the Onnenai Visitor Centre was particularly beautiful and can be done in winter with skis or snowshoes.

That night we walked into town to view the city sights — the 'seasons' statues on the bridge, the Fisherman's Wharf MOO (Marine-Our-Oasis) tourist centre, the EGG (Ever Green Garden conservatory, housing about 40 kinds of the evergreen broad-leaved trees), and the 'robata' barbecue-style bars.

This part of Hokkaido is a huge dairy area so we made sure we visited the Happiness Dairy on our way from Kushiro to our next destination. We enjoyed two scoops of ice cream each — sesame/pumpkin and potato/rhubarb-haskap. We had intended to visit the home of the Choco-Moo cheesecake that featured on Adam Liaw's TV series, but it was closed on the day we were in the area.

We also visited the Ikeda Wine Castle, home of Tokachi wines, which boasts the coldest-growing grape vines in the world. In winter when the temperature routinely gets to -20°C, the vines are buried under the ground. The Castle incorporates a research institute where they have recently developed a vine that can survive winter without being buried. Their grape varieties have been developed from native Hokkaido species of grapes. As well as the many displays inside the Castle and a small museum adjacent to the carpark, the grounds had some lovely plantings (including grape vines) as well as spectacular district views.

Photo Page 181: Mount Iwo active volcano with sulphur and white fumarolic gas

Above: Ikeda Wine Castle and Museum

Above: Lake Toro Eco-Museum; Below: Happiness Dairy, Ikeda

CHAPTER FORTY-FIVE

Farms, Foxes & Fog
Otofuke & Shinhidaka: 27–31 July

Above: Gallery Hakurin Tokachi, Nakasatsunai; Below Right: Nakasatsunai

Above & Below: House and horse stud buildings near Shinhidaka

OTOFUKE & SHINHIDAKA: 27–31 July

Farms

Our next stop was Otofuke, a town just a little east of Obihiro, where our accommodation for two nights was the Toipirka Kitaobihiro Youth Hostel, an out-of-the-way log house that was basic but comfortable. Once again we travelled along back roads through a beautiful patchwork of farms and crops as far as the eye could see.

In case you're wondering about driving in Hokkaido, Japanese people drive on the left and, as you'd expect with a low speed limit, they are very patient and courteous. And, of course, there is a zero blood alcohol limit, which seems very sensible.

We encountered many roadworks in Hokkaido. They usually use a white/red flag system to stop traffic in one direction at a time, sometimes combined with flashing/rotating lights, and always combined with lots of large arrows. The person on duty always bows as you drive past. Verge-trimming teams, conspicuous in the warm months, usually have someone holding a mesh guard to prevent whipper-snippered plants flying into traffic. You also encounter strange green boxes by the side of country roads, which hold bags of sand or salt for use in slippery snow or ice conditions. Other nice features to look out for along roads are the bridge and lamppost decorations.

Foxes

While you can't just stop by the side of the road in Japan, in Hokkaido there are frequent parking bays and rest stops (with restaurant, vending machines, information, souvenirs and toilets) along the major roads. There are also roadside signs warning you to be careful not to run over foxes or deer.

With only one full day in Otofuke we made an excellent choice to visit the Nakasatsunai Art Village and Garden, about 40 kilometres out of Obihiro. Set amongst groves of local oak trees and abundant wildflowers, it comprises five gorgeous art museums, clearings with outdoor sculptures, a large and an incredibly beautiful garden, and a restaurant in a woodland setting serving delicious, reasonably priced lunches.

Insects were abundant so we spent a lot of time ambling around taking photos. We also spotted a couple of woodpeckers and a Hokkaido squirrel (or was it perhaps a Siberian chipmunk?).

Our next stop at Shinhidaka (also called Shizunai) was located in a region whose many activities include fishing, kelp harvesting and horse breeding. On the way there, we had a brief visit to the Mount Apoi Geopark on the southern coast, a really interesting area geologically, where 'Horoman peridotite' rocks can be seen in a 'fresh state just as they had been in the earth's mantle, having hardly been altered at all' — the result of a collision between the two plates that created the Hidaka Mountains.

Fog

The following day, from our base at Shinhidaka, we returned to the Geopark for a nice walk halfway up Mount Apoi, a mountain with interesting geology, fauna and flora. The signs warned that hikers might encounter 'higuma' (brown bears), poisonous 'mamushi' (pit vipers), and 'madani' (ticks) anywhere from the foot to the top of the mountain, but also stated, understandably, that 'there is no need to be over-nervous'.

We only went half way up the mountain to the top of the forest zone because the track to the top involved a further very steep ascent of around 500 metres. Beyond the broadleaf and coniferous forest zones is a zone of alpine plants (80 species including 20 endemics) within a dwarf stone pine forest (unusual alpine flora for such a low altitude), then at the top (unusually) is a zone of birch forest. The low altitude of alpine vegetation zones is due both to the geology and the foggy climate. There was a good view, even from halfway up.

On the way back through the town of Samani we chanced upon a wonderful rotating fish drying apparatus by the roadside, so of course had to stop and take photos and movies. In Samani we also visited the Peridotite Plaza, a park dedicated to displaying rocks. The following day we drove to Sapporo via Lake Shikotsu, which was very picturesque despite the rain.

Photo Page 185: Rotating fish drying apparatus, Samani

Above: Fishing boats ready for surf launch, Samani; Below: View to sea, with Horoman peridotite in foreground, Mount Apoi

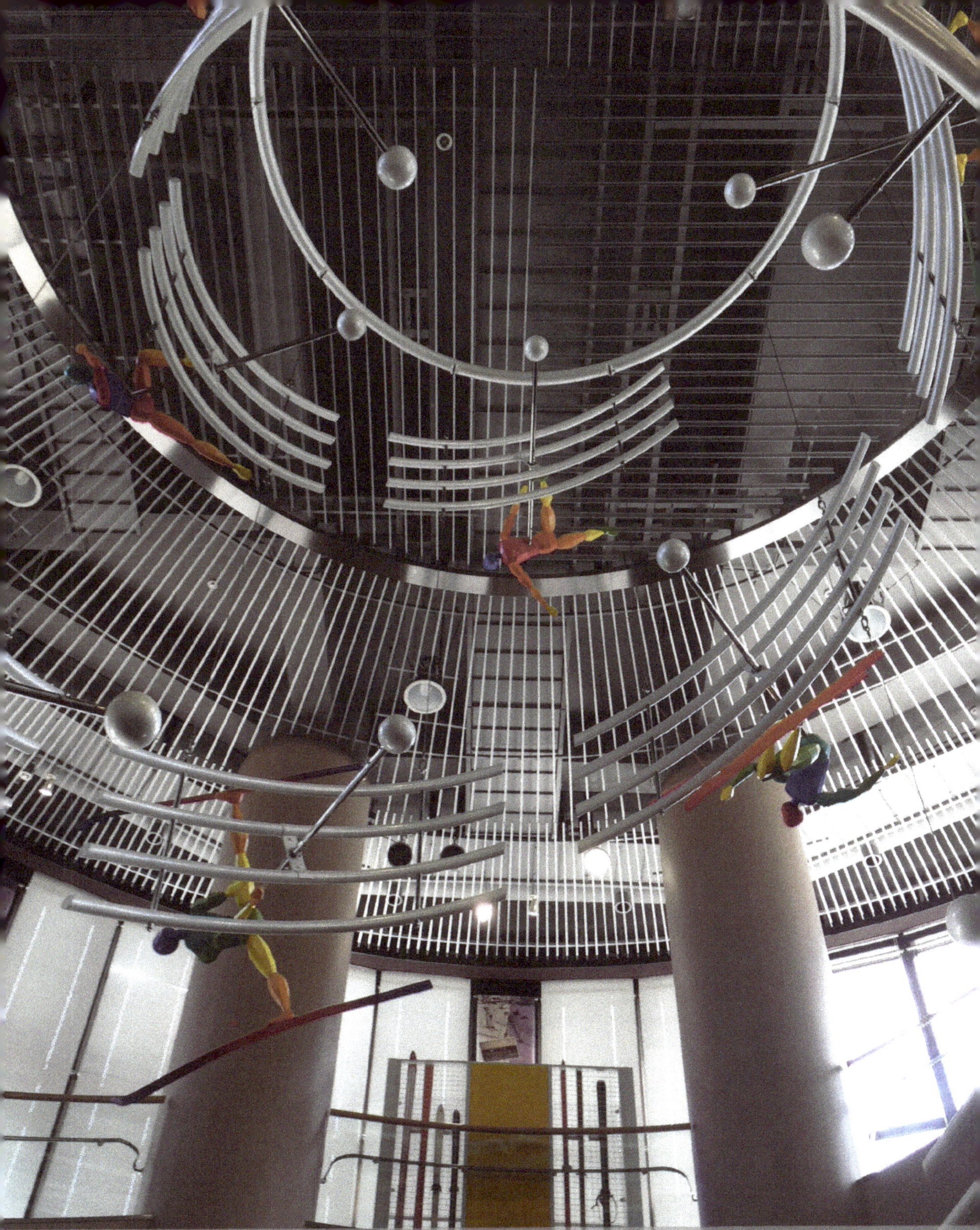

CHAPTER FORTY-SIX

TV tower, Tonden & Tozai line

Sapporo: 1–8 August

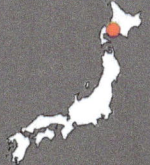

Above: Odori Park from Sapporo TV Tower

Above: Airbnb Toyohira-Ku, Sapporo

Above: Street parade, Sapporo; Below: Shikisaino-Oka flower park, Furano-Biei

SAPPORO: 1–8 August

TV tower

We returned to Sapporo for the final stage of our trip. Our Airbnb was about six kilometres from the city centre, six stops on the subway line that goes into the city via Susukino (the restaurant/entertainment area) and Odori Park. Odori Park was full of flowers and the site of a month-long summer beer festival. In winter it's the location of the world famous Snow Festival. A visit to the observation deck of the TV Tower, located in Odori Park, is a must.

There are plenty of things to do in Sapporo, and we visited Hokkaido University, the University Botanical Garden and its Ainu Museum, the Clocktower and Mount Moiwa. The latter is an observation point and winter ski field close to the city, where we skied in 1992. It was great to re-visit it in summer.

There are two huge underground shopping malls in Sapporo that intersect under Odori Park — Auroratown and Poletown — so you can shop till you drop all year long. The Sapporo Arts Festival, which is a three-yearly event, was being held at many venues throughout Sapporo through to early October. It was also the school summer holidays, so there were a lot of Sapporites and tourists visiting the city's many attractions.

Our Airbnb was interesting — two levels, each with two self-contained apartments, constructed from what appeared to be two jumbo-sized shipping containers located on the corner of a very busy intersection. On the diagonal corner was an orthopaedic hospital; across the road was a garage, a post office and a nerve and brain MRI centre; and just along from our apartment were a funeral parlour and a swimming complex. What more could you ask for?

Well, shops! And yes, the Airbnb was very handy to excellent shops in several directions, including a good supermarket near the local station and an AEON Mall in the other direction. There were also plenty of good restaurants nearby.

Tonden

After settling into the Airbnb we returned our little hire car to the office in the city just next to Sapporo Station, and the following morning collected our five visitors from the airport — a family of four American friends from Texas (who had flown in from Australia) and our teacher friend from Fukuoka.

With two shopaholics amongst the group, sightseeing took on a new, and much slower, dynamic. There are shops and souvenirs at every turn, wherever you go in Japan! One day was a shop-till-you-drop day in the city, interspersed with time in Odori Park, a visit to the TV Tower Observatory, and lunch at an Indian restaurant. Indian restaurants were a great choice for our group because of conflicting dietary requirements. We were also really fortunate in having a Tonden restaurant only 400 metres away from the Airbnb that had a delicious range of food that included Japanese and Western dishes and also suited all tastes.

We had an excellent meal at Tonden for a birthday celebration dinner the night before the visitors left. Apart from that, we mostly ate at restaurants at lunchtime because it was cheaper and easier to pick up a ready-made meal for dinner at the supermarket on the way home. There's a huge variety of fresh, delicious meals available in Japanese supermarkets.

Tozai line

One day we took an all-day bus tour to the Furano-Biei region in the centre of Hokkaido to visit two spectacular flower farms and the 'Patchwork Road' — a 26-kilometre road through rolling hills with a patchwork of various crop fields.

The winter Olympic Games were held in Sapporo in 1972 and there's a fabulous Winter Sports Museum not far from the city centre that's easy to reach on the Tozai subway line via the Maruyama Zoo. It has a lot of information about the winter Olympic Games in general, the 1972 Games in particular, and all winter sports (speed skating, curling, ice hockey, bobsleigh, among others), with really engaging interactive displays. The centrepiece of the museum is the interactive ski jump, which is not only great fun for both kids and adults alike, but imitates the real Okurayama ski jump beside the museum.

Above: Ski jump and jumper; Below Left: Interactive ski jump, Okurayama; Below Right: Sapporo Beer Festival, Odori Park

Tokyu hands, Temiya line & Takino
Sapporo & Otaru: 9–19 August

CHAPTER FORTY-SEVEN

Above: King crabs and hairy crabs, Nijo Market; Below: Glass Pyramid, Moerenuma Park

SAPPORO: 9–19 August

Tokyu Hands

A good friend from Australia who I used to work with, arrived a couple of days after our visitors from Texas and Fukuoka departed. With her, we re-visited the Winter Sports Museum (for lunch) and she and I spent a lot of time shopping in and around the city (especially at the Tokyu Hands department store). Our visitor also attended a tea ceremony in Susukino one day, and afterwards I met up with her to have a beer at the Otaru Beer Festival and visit the Nijo Fish Market, where some of the interesting items encountered were sea cucumbers (a whole shop), king crabs and hairy crabs.

Our visitor left us twice to do train trips on her own after activating her Japan Rail Pass. She was super-excited when she returned after an overnight trip to Obihiro where she had participated in the O-Bon Festival street parade and celebrations. During her stay, the three of us enjoyed many nice meals out, including another dinner at our excellent local Tonden restaurant, but as usual we mostly picked up ready-made dinners at the supermarket on our way home. There was such a choice of delicious meals that there seemed no point in cooking.

Temiya line

On one day the three of us took the train to Otaru, about an hour away on the coast. It's a lovely old city with beautiful historic buildings, an old railway line (the Temiya Line, the oldest railway in Hokkaido), a picturesque canal, a working harbour, a brewery, a huge shopping street, a steam clock, and two music box museums (one full of music boxes for sale, the other full of vintage music boxes).

In Otaru we had a delicious lunch of barbecued seafood and hot Hokkaido buttered potatoes. Otaru's famous shopping and restaurant street, Sakaimachi Street, was chock-a-block with fabulous glass shops and shops selling interesting seaweed products. Many advertised a 'husband minding' service, where your man could relax with a cup of kelp tea while you shopped without interruption or pressure.

Photo Page 193: Piano strings, installation in Glass Pyramid, Moerenuma Park

We also spent a day together at Moerenuma Park, a lovely art park some distance from the city. It has wide expanses of sculpted hillsides, a glass pyramid, lovely modern feature gardens, water features — including a swimming beach — and artworks.

Takino

While our visitor was away on her own, we did a bus trip out to Takino Suzuran Hillside National Park, the only national government park in Hokkaido. It was immense, with various types of gardens, a campground, children's playgrounds, landscaping and hectares of natural forested areas.

The children's area had a building full of climbing nets, tunnels, a castle, a hillside for rolling huge coloured balls down, two rubber hills for jumping/rolling around on, a sea of rubber, bendable 'hillocks' for climbing, a hillside of large slides, caves and rotating rock-like kaleidoscopes.

On the way home we visited the outdoor sculpture garden at Sapporo Art Park, with its hectares of beautiful and interesting sculptures set along paths in the natural forest landscape.

The weekend marked the achievement of one of our major goals of our Japan adventure. Our original aim had been to learn sufficient Japanese to be able to finish our trip in Sapporo and converse in Japanese with our long-time friends who live there and who we met through work in Sydney in the 1970s.

They were entirely responsible for us falling in love with Japan because we enjoyed our stay with them in 1992 so much that we vowed we would return for a whole year after we retired. It was wonderful to see them again after such a long time, as well as their daughter who was only a young girl when we saw her last and now has two lovely daughters of her own.

We enjoyed a delicious lunch together at Tsuruga Buffet Dining in Sapporo, with a view overlooking the Former Government Building and its gardens, and, despite not having progressed very far in our language studies, we were glad we could say a few things in Japanese.

Above: Takino Suzuran Hillside National Park

Above: Climbing nets, Takino Suzuran; Below: Children's slides, Takino Suzuran   Above: Kaleidoscope, Takino Suzuran

Snow festival, Ski jump & Stonehenge
Sapporo: 20–28 August

Above: Easter Island moai replicas at Makomanai Takino Cemetery

Above: Big Buddha, Makomanai Takino Cemetery

Above: Sapporo Dome; Below: Retractable grass pitch, Sapporo Dome

SAPPORO: 20–28 August

Snow festival

One Sunday I took a bus to Hitsujigaoka Park, which has a wonderful view over the city and the Sapporo Dome, which I also visited. Of course there was the usual mix of unusual attractions at the lookout — a statue of Dr William S Clark, symbol of the frontier spirit of Hokkaido; live sheep and sheep memorabilia commemorating the area as a former wool research centre; an Austrian House; a cafe; a huge restaurant; a lavender field (unfortunately the flowers had finished); a chapel; and the Sapporo Snow Festival Museum.

The Sapporo Dome is a beautiful fixed-roofed structure that switches between two different surfaces — an artificial turf field for baseball, and a retractable grass pitch for football games (soccer and rugby) that slides in and out of the stadium over the top of the baseball pitch. By sheer chance there was a baseball game that day, between the Hokkaido Nippon-Ham Fighters and the Saitama Seibu Lions!

Ski jump

During our last week my two school friends and their husbands arrived from Australia to stay with us in Sapporo.

We re-visited the Sapporo Winter Sports Museum and Okurayama Olympic Ski Jump — in the rain — and the Sapporo Art Park, this time visiting the large sundial, the Art Museum and Craft Buildings and enjoying a seniors' price for the buffet lunch at the Art Park Centre. With our visitors we also returned to Moerenuma Park, this time visiting the wading beach and the Sapporo Arts Festival special exhibition in the Glass Pyramid. Moerenuma Park is a vast parkland that uses eco-friendly technology and has a geometric layout of hills, fountains and play equipment such that the landscape itself a work of art.

We also enjoyed a day of shopping in the city with lunch at a noodle restaurant that also had gyu-don (beef and egg on rice), edamame beans and chips, and dinner at our fabulous local restaurant Tonden.

Photo Page 197: Making noodles at restaurant, Paseo, Sapporo Station

When all our guests had gone, our packing was in order and the Airbnb cleaned up, we made the most of our last day in Sapporo to visit the Makomanai Takino Cemetery, which we had noticed from the bus on our return from Takino Suzuran Hillside National Park. We had hoped to go to the big illumination event being held at Takino Suzuran that night but there seemed to be no way to get home by public transport late at night.

Stonehenge

Makomanai is such a huge area that you can't see the actual cemetery (which itself is a huge and beautiful working cemetery) until you walk a fair way past Stonehenge. Yes, the park has full-scale replicas, not only of Stonehenge, but also of the Easter Island moai statues, assorted sphinxes, Mayan jaguars, and an enormous statue of Buddha as its centrepiece. The statue is set almost entirely underground with only the top of its head poking up from the Hill of the Buddha, an extraordinary creation by architect Tadao Ando planted with thousands of lavender bushes. Like the Sapporo Art Park and nearby national park, you can hire cross-country skis and snowshoes to view the artworks in winter.

We had an absolutely wonderful year in Japan. Arriving home in Australia was bound to be a culture shock!

Gluten-Free Travel in Japan

In his mid-50s Bill was diagnosed with coeliac disease. Nowadays in Australia there is a wealth of gluten-free products available and people are aware of this food allergy. Most advice for travelling in Japan for those who are coeliac is 'don't'. The relevant genes are virtually non-existent in the Japanese population, so few Japanese people are coeliac and gluten-free products aren't commonly available. This provided us with an extra challenge, however we managed to find suitable foods for Bill to eat.

Gluten-Free Travel in Japan is the title of my accompanying book on Japan. It's full of all the food photos I didn't have room to include in this book! You'll find out how to do it, where to buy foods, what to ask for, and the best places to eat out.

Above: Craft Hall, Ceramic Studio and Wood Crafts studio, Sapporo Art Park

Above: Sculpture Garden, Sapporo Art Park; Below: Sapporo Art Museum

Map showing main locations mentioned in text

PRACTICAL TIPS & ADVICE

Adaptors
Voltage in Japan is 100V and you'll need a plug with two straight pins.

Alcohol
Beer is similar in price to Australia; spirits, wines, sake and shochu are cheaper than in Australia.

Booking accommodation
Accommodation websites such as booking.com are reliable and easy to use. All Airbnbs listed in Japan have to be accredited and so are reliable.

Booking entertainment or sports
Use vending machines at convenience stores where the staff will be happy to help you. Book seats for sumo touraments through the English online website, as soon as bookings open; chair seating is available in the upper rows but sells out quickly.

Booking transport
Look up train timetables online or search for routes in Google Maps. Make a list of the trains you want to catch and show the list at a Japan Rail ticket counter where they will issue the tickets.

Budgeting
Our budget was $300 per day for two people, all inclusive of accommodation, transport and meals.

Clothes
Pack light and choose clothing appropriate for the season. Layers of clothing are best if moving in and out of heated public transport, stores or houses. Clothes are quite expensive to buy in Japan, and might not be available in larger sizes. Take your own.

Currency & credit cards
The Japanese currency is the yen. Cash is still the preferred payment method, and big bills are usually accepted, although you'll need coins for storage lockers and buses generally do not accept bills above 1000 yen. Cash is best for entrance fees at tourist venues, small restaurants and shops. Credit cards are usually accepted in hotels, department stores, larger restaurants, convenience stores and supermarkets. IC cards, used mainly for transport, can also be used for payment in many places.

Driving
Japanese drive on the left hand side, though they usually walk on the right hand side. If you intend to drive in Japan, you will need an International Driver's Licence. If you hire a car in Japan, make sure you request an English language 'navi'. Car hire costs are similar to Australia.

Earthquakes & tsunamis
Download the 'Safety tips' application to receive early warnings and advisories of disasters and weather warnings. Available in many different languages. Register with the Australian Department of Foreign Affairs (or equivalent) before leaving.

Emergency phone numbers
Phone 119 for fire and ambulance. Phone 110 for police.

Etiquette
There are many rules of etiquette that foreign visitors should be aware of before visiting Japan. There is a wealth of information online.

Events
There are many events, festivals and public holidays in Japan, so it's a good idea to check them out online. It may be hard to find accommodation during peaks of cherry blossom and autumn foliage, or in Golden Week or O-Bon. On the other hand you may wish to plan your visit around these events.

Garbage & recycling
Most accommodation other than hotels will require you to separate your garbage into three, or up to fourteen, different categories for recycling — such as paper/cardboard, PET bottles, glass, aluminium.

Internet, wi-fi, data
Most types of accommodation provide wi-fi or mobile wi-fi. You can rent your own mobile wi-fi by booking online and picking up a device at the airport on arrival. Handy for using Google Maps and Google Translate while on the move.

Japan Rail Passes
Japan Rail Passes make train travel very economical if you are doing a lot of travelling in a short time,

especially if you're using shinkansens. Available as 7-day, 14-day or 21-day options, ordinary class or green (first) class. Buy online at least seven days before you leave. Also available at Tokyo Station. Major stations have a ticket counter especially for Rail Pass bookings, with English-speaking staff.

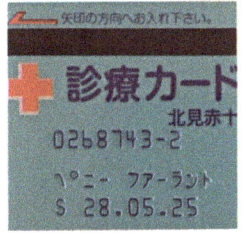

Language

Japanese is a very difficult language to learn. However, railway station signage includes names in romaji (English alphabet) for previous, current and next stops. Google Translate is helpful, but not perfect, especially for reading labels.

Laundry

Laundromats (coin laundries) are abundant in Japan. They have a wide range of washers, dryers, and also change machines. Note that some machines add the laundry powder automatically. Most types of accommodation, including hotels, have coin-operated washers and dryers available for guests to use.

Luggage

Travel light, there's not a lot of room for large bags on trains and few very large storage lockers at stations. The luggage forwarding system for sending luggage from one hotel to the next is excellent.

Medical & hospitals

If you want to take more than a month's worth of medicines into Japan, you will need to fill out a 'yakkan shoumei' (medicine importation) form, have it approved by email before you leave, and present it at immigration on the way in. Check online for banned drugs such as pseudoephedrine.

The Japanese medical system doesn't work by referrals from general practitioners. If you are unwell, it's best to go to a large hospital (with many different departments) or directly to the relevant specialist clinic (e.g. ear-nose and throat, orthopedic, etc.). Without a Japanese health card you will have to pay upfront. However, the costs are reasonable and the system is efficient.

The clinic or hospital will prescribe medicines and the pharmacy will usually get an English speaker on the phone to check your medical history and explain dosages. You should be able to claim on your travel insurance.

Mobile phones & laptops

Use your own mobile phone but be careful of roaming charges. Or select a plan that charges a flat fee for 24 hours if activated. Or rent a phone. SIM cards are usually for data only, not voice calls. Phone cards for public phones are available at convenience stores.

Onsens

Onsens or spa baths are places to relax. They may be indoor or outdoor or a mixture of both. They are usually separate for men and women, and strict procedures and etiquette must be observed (check online). Most onsens don't accept visitors with tattoos due to an old association with organised crime.

Seniors discounts

In Japan, older people qualify as Seniors at either 65 or 70 years of age, depending on the place. Usually the discounts only apply to residents, and sometimes only to residents of the immediate local government area. Some major attractions offer discounts for overseas tourists with appropriate passports.

Tea, coffee, hot chocolate

Plenty of options are available as hot and cold drinks from vending machines and convenience stores. Tea and coffee are usually available in either black or white, and most are sweetened. However you'll find other styles of coffee like cappucinos and lattes at cafes like Starbucks. Instant and drip coffee bags are available from supermarkets.

Transport cards

IC cards, such Suica, Nimoca and Icoca, are stored-value cards used primarily for public transport. Most cards, no matter where they are purchased, can be used Japan-wide.

Visas

You won't need to obtain a visa before you travel to Japan, as 90-day tourist visas are issued upon arrival. If you intend to stay longer, the easiest option is to leave the country (e.g. go to South Korea) and return a short time later. Six-month sightseeing visas are available but require a lot of paperwork. They can be renewed for a further six months while in Japan, within three months of the expiry date.

Water

Tap water is safe to drink throughout Japan.

Weather

Japan experiences typhoons from July to October, especially in August and September. Expect snow in winter as far south as Kyushu, with rail and road closures further north.

Index

A

ABASHIRI 171, 175
    Abashiri Prison Museum 175
    Koshimizu Natural Flower Garden 175
    Lake Abashiri 175
    Moyoro Shell Mound Museum 175, 176
    Museum of Northern Peoples 175
    Okhotsk Ryu-hyo Museum 175
    Sea of Okhotsk 175
    Tofutsu-ko Waterfowl & Wetland Centre 175
Accommodation 7, 11, 31, 115, 202
    Airbnbs 27, 35, 39, 51, 55, 59, 79, 83, 91, 95, 99, 135, 139, 147, 155, 167, 190, 191, 199, 202
        Coco House, Miyazu 99
    Guest Houses 35
        Guest House Asora, Aso Town 70, 71
        Guest House Hooju, Aoshima 71
        Guest House Yasumizaka, Kushiro 183
    Hostels 123
        Grids Hostel & Hostel, Sapporo 166, 167
        K's House Hostels 43, 103, 107, 119, 123, 131
    Hotels 202
        Benesse House, Naoshima 39, 40
        Hotel Avan, Sukumo 87
        Hotel Remm, Kagoshima 79
        Sunlife Hotel, Hakata 43
    Ryokans
        Ryokan Yunomineso 31
    Youth Hostels 39, 47, 63, 163, 187
        Kurashiki Youth Hostel 39
        Saga Youth Hostel 43
        Toipirka Kitaobihiro Youth Hostel, Otofuke 187
        Youth Hostel Murataya Ryokan, Takamori 47
Adaptors (Power) 202
Ainu 6, 167, 191
    Ainu Museum, Hokkaido University, Sapporo 191
    Kaneto Ainu Museum, Asahikawa 166
Airbnbs See Accommodation
Akan Mashu National Park, Hokkaido 183
    Wakoto Peninsula 183
AKITA 155
    Akita Museum of Art 155
    Annual Events in Akita 155
    Fujita Tsuguharu (Artist) 155
AKUNE 79
Alcoholic Drinks
    Beer 19, 31, 127, 202
    Sake (Rice Wine) 31, 35, 79, 202
    Spirits 202
        Awamori 55, 59
        Shochu 19, 202
        Whiskey 55, 127
    Wine 202
        Plum Wine 31
        Tokachi Wines 183
Alpine Plants 187
AMANOHASHIDATE 98, 99
    Kasamatsu Park 100
    Pine Forest 99
Ambulance 202
Animal Cafes 119
Animatronics 79, 139
Anime 96
AOSHIMA 71
    Aoshima Island 72
    Aoshima Shrine 72
    Giant's Washboard 71, 72
    Guest House Hooju 71
    Miyako Botanic Garden 71
Aquaria See Zoos & Aquariums

Argonaut 67
ARITA 43
    Kyushu Ceramic Museum 44
Art Galleries See Museums & Art Galleries
Art Islands 39
ASAHIKAWA 166, 167, 171
    Asahiyama Zoo 166, 167
    Daisetsuzan National Park 167
    Kaneto Ainu Museum 166, 167
Ashizuri Mizaki See Cape Ashizuri
Ashizuri-Uwakai National Park, Shikoku 87
ASO TOWN 71
    Guest House Asora 71
Australian Department of Foreign Affairs 202
Autumn Foliage 202

B

Barge 100
Barns 170, 175
Baseball 126, 199
Bears 175, 178, 179, 187
Beech Forest 158
Beer See Alcoholic Drinks
Beni-Imo See Vegetables, Purple Sweet Potatoes
Bento Boxes 127
BEPPU 67
    Hells 67
        Onishibouzu Jigoku 68
        Umi Jigoku 68
    Takegawara Onsen 67, 68
    Umitamago Aquarium 66, 67
Best Foreign Film 159
Bicycles 99, 151
Black Flies 179
Blowfish 115
Blue Poppies 167, 168
Boardwalk 171, 178, 179
Boats 171
    Boat Building 88
Bonsai 135
Bookshop 15
Boxing Day 55
Buckwheat 147
Buddhism 19, 31, 35
    Buddha 11, 135, 198
    Daibutsu Great Buddha, Ushiku 111
Budget 7
Burial Mound 39

C

Calligraphy 59, 83, 118, 119, 159
Camellias 87
Cape Ashizuri (Ashizuri Mizaki) 86, 87
    Curvature of the Earth 86
    Hakusan Natural Arch 87
    John Manjiro 87
        John Manjiro Foot Spa 87
        John Manjiro Statue 87
    Kongofukuji Temple 86, 87
        Rock Garden 86
Cape Kiritappu 183

Cape Maeda 59

Cape Manzamo 59

Cape Muroto 94, 95
   Hotsumisaki Temple 95
   Shintaro Nakaoka Statue 94

Cape Noshappu 171

Cape Soya 171
   Tower of Prayer for Korean Airlines Flight 007 172

Car Hire 202

Cars 43
   Car Hire 67, 167, 191

Castles
   Hikone Castle 114
   Himeji Castle 27, 28
     White Heron Main Keep 27
   Hirosaki Castle 155
   Hiroshima Castle 43
   Kochi Castle 91
   Kumamoto Castle 46, 47
   Kyoto Castle (Nijo-Jo) 103, 107, 108
   Matsuyama Castle 83
   Osaka Castle 27
   Shurijo Castle, Naha 55
   Tokushima Castle 96
   Yamagata Castle 159
   Yuzuki Castle Ruins, Matsuyama 83

Caves 59
   Cave Mailbox 59

Ceramic Dolls 71

Ceramics 43

Cezanne 159

Chagall 131, 159

Cherry Blossom (Sakura) 95, 103, 107, 115, 118, 119, 202

Cherry-Picking 167

Chicken
   Charcoal Chicken 87
   Chicken Necks 87
   Chicken Sashimi 39
   Chicken Skewers 43
   Yakitori (Chicken Skewers) 19, 39, 139

Chinkabashi (Submersible Bridges) 87, 91, 92

Chocolate Bananas 115

Christmas Day 55

Christmas Lights 43

Clams 171

Clothes 202

Commerson's Dolphins 36

Convenience Stores (Konbini) 7, 71, 202, 203

Cooking Classes 11
   Ramen 15

Cow Lillies 179, 180

Crabs 171, 194, 195

Cranes 79, 183
   Crane Observation Centre, Izumi 78

Credit Cards 202

Currency 202
   Yen 202

Curries 183

D

Daisetsuzan National Park, Hokkaido 167
   Daisetsu Mori no Garden 167
   Momojidani Waterfall 167, 168
   Mount Kurodake 167
   Sounkyo Gorge 167
   Sounkyo Onsen 167

Data 202

Degas 159

Dentist 83

Department of Immigration 67

Department Stores 202

Departures (Movie) 159

Dinners 23

Dosages 203

Drinks (Non-Alcoholic)
   Coffee
     Drip Coffee Bags 203

Driving 7, 187, 202

Dr William S Clark 199

E

Earthquakes 22, 46, 47, 83, 111, 131, 202
   Kobe Earthquake 111

Edo Period 19, 27, 115, 123, 139

Egg-Vending Machine 94, 95

Eidelweiss 171, 172

Ema (Wooden Plaques) 123, 163

Emergency Phone Numbers 202

Entertainment 202

Etiquette 202

Events 202

Expressways 167

F

Fake Foods 19
   Fake Food Workshop Riki 19, 20

Farms 187

Ferries 74, 75, 83, 171

Festivals 202
   O-Bon 202

Festivals & Holidays 143
   Emperor's Birthday 59
   Golden Week 131
   Hojoya Festival, Fukuoka 11, 12
   Naked Man Festival (Saidaiji Eyo), Okayama 79, 80
   Neputa Festival, Hirosaki 155
   Respect for the Aged Day 15
   Sanja Festival, Tokyo 139, 140
   Shirone Kite Festival 150
   Snow Festival, Sapporo 7, 191, 199
   Takayama Festival Floats Exhibition Hall 142, 143

Fire 23, 83, 202

Fish
   Fish Drying Apparatus 187
   Fishing Boats 188
   Fishing Nets 170
   Flying Fish 74, 75, 171
   Sweet Fish 43, 115, 143

Fog 171, 183

Food Drying Racks 88

Football 199

Foxes 171, 187

Frank Gehry 111

Frank Lloyd Wright 162, 163

Fruit 11, 14, 18, 19
   Bankan (large citrus) 79
   Musk Melon 19
   Yuzu 91

FUKUOKA 11, 15, 19, 22, 23, 27, 43, 67, 131, 195
   Camp Hakata Restaurant 67

Dazaifu 23
Fukuoka Citizens' Disaster Prevention Centre 22, 23
Fukuoka Dome 23
Fukuoka Tower 23
Furukawa Cooking School 11
Hakata 11, 43
   Sunlife Hotel 43
Hakata Doll (Ningyo) Painting 11
Hakozakigu Shrine 11
Hojoya Festival 11, 12
Ijiri 14
Itoshima Beach 23
Kasuga 12, 14, 15, 16, 23, 24
Kasugabaru 19
Kurume 23
Kyushu National Museum 22, 23
Local Historical Museum 15
Nanzoin Temple 11
NILS Language School 24
Ohashi 14
Open-Top Bus 15
Shikanoshima 23, 24
Tenjin 15
Tenmangu Shrine 23
Yaburekabure Restaurant 19
Yanagawa 19, 20
Yayoi Bus 20
Yayoi Hundred Yen Community Buses 20

Fumaroles 131, 183

Furano-Biei, Hokkaido 191
   Shikisaino-Oka Flower Park 190

G

Garbage 202

Gardens & Parks 7, 87, 136
   Arashiyama Hills Bamboo Path, Kyoto 106, 107
   Arboretum Churaumi, Okinawa 52
   Ashikaga Flower Park 126, 127
   Borrowed Scenery 110, 111
   Central Park, Tokushima 95
   Daisetsu Mori no Garden, Hokkaido 168
   Denboin Garden, Tokyo 123
   Flower Road Park, Kobe 111, 112
   Fujita Memorial Garden, Hirosaki 154, 155
   Furano-Biei, Hokkaido 191
   Glover Garden, Nakasaki 47
   Hakone Botanical Garden of Wetlands 131, 132
   Hakusan Koen Park, Niigata 151
   Hibiya Park, Tokyo 123, 124
   Higashi-Yuenchi Park, Kobe 111
   Himeji Castle Nishi-Oyashiki-Ato (Koen-en) Garden 27
   Hirosaki Castle Botanical Garden 155
   Hiroshima Peace Park 43
   Hitachi Seaside Park 127, 128
   Hitsujigaoka Park, Sapporo 199
   Hojo Garden, Kyoto 103
   Hokkaido University Botanical Garden, Sapporo 191
   Isuien Garden, Nara 110, 111
   Kasamatsu Park, Amanohashidate 100
   Koraku-en, Okayama 39, 79
   Koshimizu Natural Flower Garden, Hokkaido 175, 176
   Kumamoto Zoo/Botanical Gardens 47
   Makino Botanical Garden, Kochi 91
   Meriken Park Earthquake Memorial Park and Harbor Land, Yokohama 111
   Miyako Botanic Garden, Aoshima 71
   Moerenuma Park, Sapporo 194, 195, 199
   Mount Apoi Geopark, Hokkaido 187
   Nakasatsunai Art Village Garden, Hokkaido 187
   Nikko Botanical Garden 163
   Ninomaru Historical Garden, Matsuyama 82, 83
   Odori Park, Sapporo 191, 192
   Okayama Koraku-en 38
   Onshi-Hakone Koen, Hakone 131
   Palace East Gardens, Tokyo 119, 139
   Peace Memorial Park, Okinawa 54, 55
   Peace Park, Nagasaki 46
   Ritsurin Garden, Takamatsu 38, 39
      Nighttime Illuminations 39
   Rock Garden Kongofukuji Temple, Cape Ashizuri 86
   Ryoanji Rock Garden, Kyoto 107
   Sapporo Art Park 195, 199
   Sengan-en Garden, Kagoshima 78, 79
   Shikisaino-Oka Flower Park, Furano-Biei, Hokkaido 190
   Shosei-en Garden, Kyoto 107
   Soraku-en Garden, Kobe 111

Suizenji Jojuen, Kumamoto 46, 47
Sumida Park, Tokyo 118, 119
Takamori Tunnel Park 47
Tazawako Heart Herb Garden 159
Togakushi Forest Botanical Garden, Nagano 147
Tokyo Institute for Nature Study 122, 123
Tosa Dog Park, Kochi 91
Tsukiyama (Mountain Replicas) 47
Tsuruoka Park 151
Tsutenkyo Bridge Garden, Kyoto 102, 103
Ueno Park, Tokyo 119
Ushiku Daibutsu, Tokyo 135
Yokohama Garden Necklace 126, 127
Yoshikien Garden, Nara 111

Geisha 107

Geta 103

Gingko 43

Google Maps 27, 202

Google Translate 202, 203

Gunkanjima 47

Gyu-Don (Beef Bowl) 199

H

Habu (Snake) 59

Haiku 79, 83, 84

Haircuts 167

HAKONE 130, 131, 132, 135
   Hakone 3-Day Free Pass 131
   Hakone Botanical Garden of Wetlands 131, 132
   Hakone-Fuji 3-Day Free Pass 131
   Hakone Open Air Sculpture Museum 130, 131
   Key Hiraga Museum 132
   Lalique Museum 131
   Narukawa Art Museum 130, 131
   Onshi-Hakone Koen 131
   Owakudani 131
   Pola Museum of Art 131
   Ropeway 131

Halloween 23, 26, 27

HAMANAKA 183

Hamazushi Sushi Restaurant 11, 12

Hana-Temari Restaurant 43

Hashima See Gunkanjima

Henry Moore 131

Hidaka Mountains 187

HIMEJI 27
   Himeji Castle 27, 28
   Himeji Castle Nishi-Oyashiki-Ato (Koen-en) Garden 27

HIROSAKI 155
   Arts and Handcrafts Centre 155
   Fujita Memorial Garden 154, 155
   Hirosaki Castle 155
   Hirosaki Castle Botanical Garden 155
   Neputa Festival 155

HIROSHIMA 42, 43
   Atomic Bomb Dome 42, 43
   Hiroshima Castle 43
   Hiroshima Peace Park 43
   Mazda Museum 43, 44
   Peace Memorial Museum 43

Hoba Miso 143

HOKKAIDO 167, 171, 175, 183, 187, 195, 199
   Akan Mashu National Park 183
   Daisetsu Mori no Garden 168
   Furano-Biei 191
   Kiritappu Coast 182
   Koshimizu Natural Flower Garden 175, 176
   Kushiro-Shitsugen National Park 183
   Lake Toro Eco-Museum 184
   Mount Apoi Geopark 187
   Notsuke Peninsula 179
   Onneto Hot Waterfall 182, 183

Patchwork Road 191
　　Rishiri Rebun Sarobetsu National Park 171
　　Shibetsu Salmon Museum 179
　　Shikisaino-Oka Flower Park, Furano-Biei 190
　　Taiho Koki Sumo Museum 183
　　Tofutsu Lake Bird Observatory 175

HONSHU 39, 99, 103, 119
　　Tokyo
　　　　Tokyo Station 203

Horoman Peridotite 187, 188

Horse Studs 186

Hospital 35

Hostels See Accommodation

Hotels See Accommodation

Hot-Pots (Nabe, Shabu-Shabu) 43, 71, 135, 139, 171
　　Bishunabe (Chicken & Vegetable Hot-Pot) 43

Hot Sand Baths 68

Husband Minding 195

I

IC Cards 203
　　Icoca 203
　　Nimoca 203
　　Suica 203

Icecream 143, 147

Ice Fishing 175

Ice Walls 146

Ichigo no Sato Strawberry Farm 127, 128

Ikebana 19
　　Food Ikebana 90, 91

IKEDA 184
　　Happiness Dairy 183, 184
　　Ikeda Wine Castle 183
　　Ikeda Wine Museum 183, 184

IMARI 43

Inakazushi 87

Inari (Foxes) 103

Inland Sea 95

International Driver's Licence 202

Internet 202

ISE 31, 32, 35
　　Geku (Toyouke Dai-Jingu) Outer Shrine 31, 35
　　Ise Grand Shrine (Ise Jingu) 31, 35
　　Naiku (Kotai Jingu), Inner Shrine 35

ITOMAN 51, 54, 59, 60
　　Bibi Beach 55
　　Cornerstone of Peace 54
　　Growers' Market 51, 55
　　Itoman City Market 51, 56
　　Itoman Farm 55
　　Itoman Fish Centre 51, 55
　　Itoman Peaceful Illuminations 54, 55
　　Masahiro Brewery 55

Iwataya Department Store 18, 19

IYA VALLEY 99
　　Biwa-no-Take Waterfall 99
　　Chiourii 99
　　Heike Folklore House 99
　　Hotel Nanoyado 99
　　Kazura-Bashi Vine Bridge 98
　　Nishi-Iya 99
　　Obuke 99
　　Peeing Boy Statue 99

Izakaya 18, 19, 107

IZUMI 79
　　Crane Observation Centre 79

J

James Bond 31, 47

Japanese Alps 143, 147

Japan National Tourism Organisation 103, 107

Japan Post 67

Japan Rail Pass 7, 11, 195

Japan Rail Passes 202

Jellyfish 151

K

Kabuki 83, 84, 119

KAGOSHIMA 71, 75, 79
　　Hotel Remm 79
　　Museum of the Meiji Restoration 78, 79
　　　　Saigo Takamori 78
　　Sakurajima 78, 79
　　Sengan-en Garden 78, 79

Kaida Horses 115

Kaldi Coffee Farm 15

Kaleidoscopes 131, 195, 196

KAMINOYAMA 159

KARATSU 43

KASHIKOJIMA 35

Katsuo no Tataki (Seared Bonito Sashimi) 87

Katsushika Hokusai (Woodblock Artist) 139

Kazura-Bashi (Vine Bridge) 99

Kazuyo Sejima (Architect) 151

Ken-Do (Samurai Training) 163

Kentucky Fried Chicken 55, 127

Kettle Steamed Rice 83

Key Hiraga (Artist) 131

Kimono Hire 103, 104, 107

Kinjo Meiko (Potter) 51

KITAMI 175

Kitchen Equipment 151

Kites 151

KOBE 111, 112
　　Chinese Kantel-byo Mausoleum 111, 112
　　Flower Road Park 111, 112
　　Foreign Settlement Area 111
　　Higashi-Yuenchi Park 111
　　Honganji Kobe Betsuin Temple 111
　　Rough Rare Restaurant 111
　　Soraku-en Garden 111
　　Venus Bridge 111

KOCHI 91, 95
　　Chikurinji Temple 91
　　Katsurahama Beach 91
　　Kochi Castle 91
　　Kochi Sunday Market 91
　　Makino Botanical Garden 91
　　Sakamoto Ryoma Memorial Museum 91
　　Tosa Dog Park 91
　　Tosa No Ikyaku 91

Komekara (Deep Fried Chicken) 43

Kon Kaneo (Kokeshi Doll Teacher) 155

Kotai-Jingu See ISE, Grand Ise Shrine, Naiku

KOYASAN 31
　　Kongobuji 31
　　Oku-no-in Cemetery 31

KUMAMOTO 47
　　Kumamon 47
　　Kumamoto Castle 46, 47
　　Kumamoto Zoo/Botanical Gardens 47

Suizenji Jojuen 47
KUMANO-KODO PILGRIMAGE 7, 31 See also Shrines & Temples
  Hashimoto 31
  Hongu Taisha Shrine 31, 35
  Ise 31
  Kii Katsura 31
  Koguchi 31
  Nachi Taisha Shrine 30, 31
  Nakanoshima 31
  Ryokan Yunomineso 31
  Shingu Shrine 31
  Takahara 31
  Takajiri-Oji 31
  Tsugizajura-Oji 31
  Yunomine Onsen 30, 31

KURAMA 107

KURASHIKI 39, 79
  Bikan Historical Area 38
  Kurashiki Youth Hostel 39

KUROISHI 155
  Kokeshi Dolls 154, 155, 156
  Tanbo-Art 155, 156

KUSHIRO 6, 183
  Akan Mashu National Park 183
  Cape Kiritappu 183
  EGG (Ever Green Garden conservatory) 183
  Guest House Yasumizaka 183
  Kushiro-Shitsugen National Park 183
  Marimo Algae Balls 182, 183
  Marine-Our-Oasis (MOO) 183
  Onnenai Visitor Centre 183

Kushiro-Shitsugen National Park, Hokkaido 183
  Lake Toro Eco-Museum 183

KYOTO 98, 99, 103, 104, 107, 111, 119
  Arashiyama Hills Bamboo Path 106, 107
  Eizen Railway 107
  Fushimi-Inari Shrine 102, 103
  Ginkakuji Silver Temple 103
  Gion Geisha District 107
  Higashi Honganji Temple 107
  Hojo Garden 103
  Imperial Palace 106, 107
  JR Railway Museum 103
  Keihan Railway 107
  Kinkakuji Golden Temple 106, 107
  Kyoto Castle (Nijo-Jo) 103, 107, 108
  Kyoto Railway Museum 102
  Kyoto Station 99
  Lake Biwa Aqueduct Museum 103
  Mount Inari 102
  Nanzenji Temple 103, 104
  Nishi Honganji Temple 107
  Philosophers Walk 103, 104
  Pontocho 107
  Ryoanji Rock Garden 107
  Ryoanji Temple 107
  Sanjusangendo Temple & Hall 107, 108
  Sennyuji Temple 103
  Shosei-en Garden 107
  Tofukuji Temple 103
  Toji Temple 103, 107, 108
  Tsutenkyo Bridge Garden 102, 103

Kyoto & Vicinity Walking Guide 103, 107

KYUSHU 43, 51, 71, 103, 167, 203
  Yakushima National Park 75

L

Lacquerware 50, 51, 143, 155

Lake Akan 182, 183
  Marimo Algae Balls 183

Lake Ashi 130, 131

Lake Kussharo 183
  Wakoto Peninsula 183

Lake Mashu 182, 183

Lake Onneto 183

Lake Rausu 180

Lake Shikotsu 187

Lake Tazawako 158, 159

Language 203
  Language School 11
  NILS 15, 24

Laundry & Laundromats 147

Lawson Station 127

Lonely Planet 71, 95

Luggage 11, 67, 203
  Luggage Forwarding 203

M

Macaques (Monkeys) 67, 75

Maglev 35

Magnolias 143

Manatees 35

Map 201

Maps.me 27

Marimo Algae Balls 182, 183

Matisse 159

Matsuri See Festivals & Holidays

MATSUYAMA 83, 87
  Botchan Karaduri Clock 83
  Dogo Onsen Honkan 83
  Matsuyama Castle 83
  Mitsu 82, 83
    Mitsu Morning Market 83
  Ninomaru Historical Garden 82, 83
  Taisanji Temple 82, 83
  Yuzuki Castle Ruins, Matsuyama 83

Medical 203
  Hospitals 203
  Medical History 203
  Medicines 203

Mikan Mochi 35

Milk Road, Hokkaido 170

Minamiaso Mizuno-Umareru-Sato Hakusui-Kogen Station 47

Minatogawa Man 59

Mirror Lake 151

Miso Fish 83

Miso Soup 171

Mitsu See MATSUYAMA

Mitsubishi 47

MIYAJIMA 42, 43
  Itsukushima Shrine 43
  Miyajima 'Floating' Shrine 42, 43

MIYAMURA 98
  Miyamura Station 99

MIYAZAKI 71

MIYAZU 99
  Amanohashidate 100
  Coco House 99
  Miyamura Station 99

Mobile Phone 203

Mobile Wi-Fi 202

Mochi (Sweet Rice Balls) 66, 67

MONBETSU 171, 174, 175
  Big Snow Crab Claw 174
  Icebreaker Trips 175
  Okhotsk Sea Ice Museum 175
  Sea Angels 175
  Seal Rehabilitation Facility 175
  Sea of Okhotsk 175

Monet 39, 159

Mount Apoi 188
  Mount Apoi Geopark 187

Mount Aso 47, 48, 70, 71
  Caldera 70, 71
  Daikanbo 70, 71
  Super Ring 71
  Volcano Museum 71

Mount Fuji 11, 46, 130, 131

Mount Haguro 151

Mount Iwo 183

Mount Kurodake 168

Mount Misen 42, 43

Mount Moiwa 191

Mount Rishiri 172

Mount Sanpokojin 160

Mount Takao 119, 120
  Takaosan Yakuoin Temple 119

MUGI 95
  Mollusca Mugi 95

Muroto Mizaki See Cape Muroto

Museums & Art Galleries 7, 187, 195
  Abashiri Prison Museum 175
  Ainu Museum, Hokkaido University, Sapporo 191
  Akita Museum of Art 155
  Benesse House Museum of Art, Naoshima 39
  Chichu Museum, Naoshima 39
  Chidokan Clan School, Tsuruoka 151
  Chido Museum, Naoshima 151
  Drum Museum, Tokyo 119
  Gunkanjima Digital Museum, Nagasaki 47
  Hakone Open Air Sculpture Museum 130, 131
  Heike Folklore House, Iya Valley 99
  Hida Takayama Museum of Art 143, 144
  History & Folklore Museum, Museum of Commercial & Domestic Life, Uchiko 83
  Ikazaki Kite Museum, Uchiko 83
  Ikeda Wine Museum 183, 184
  Japan Folk Crafts Museum and West Hall, Tokyo 139
  JR Railway Museum, Nagoya 34, 35
  Kaneto Ainu Museum, Asahikawa 166, 167
  Key Hiraga Museum, Hakone 131, 132
  Kyoto Railway Museum 102
  Kyushu Ceramic Museum, Arita 44
  Kyushu National Museum, Fukuoka 22, 23
  Lake Biwa Aqueduct Museum, Kyoto 103
  Lake Toro Eco-Museum, Hokkaido 184
  Lalique Museum, Hakone 131
  Lee Ufan Museum, Naoshima 39
  Local Historical Museum, Kasuga, Fukuoka 15
  Maritime Museum, Yokohama 111
  Mazda Museum, Hiroshima 43, 44
  Mollusca Mugi 95
  Moyoro Shell Mound Museum, Abashiri 175, 176
  Museum of Northern Peoples, Abashiri 175
  Museum of Oriental Ceramics, Osaka 26, 27
  Museum of the Meiji Restoration, Kagoshima 78, 79
    Saigo Takamori 78
  Nagasaki Peace Museum 47
  Nagoya City Science Museum 34, 35
  Nakasatsunai Art Village, Otofuke 186, 187
    Gallery Hakurin Tokachi 186
  Narukawa Art Museum, Hakone 130, 131
  National Art Centre, Tokyo 123
  National Museum of Modern Art & Crafts Annex, Tokyo 123, 139
  Niigata Manga Animation Museum 150, 151
  Niigata Sake Museum 151, 152
  Okada Museum of Art, Hakone 130, 131
  Okhotsk Ryu-hyo Museum, Abashiri 175
  Okhotsk Sea Ice Museum, Monbetsu 175
  Okumura Museum, Nara 111
  Okurayama Winter Sports Museum, Sapporo 191, 192, 195, 199
  Omiya Bonsai Art Museum 135, 139
  Parasitology Museum, Tokyo 122
  Peace Memorial Museum, Hiroshima 43
  Pola Museum of Art, Hakone 131
  Ryogoku Kokugikan Sumo Stadium Museum, Tokyo 119
  Saga Hot-Air Balloon Museum 44

  Saitama Railway Museum 138, 139
  Sakamoto Ryoma Memorial Museum, Kochi 91
    Sakamoto Ryoma (Samurai) 91
  Sapporo Art Museum & Craft Buildings 199, 200
  Sapporo Art Park 195, 199, 200
  Sapporo Snow Festival Museum 199
  Shibetsu Salmon Museum 179
  Shirakawa-go, Takayama 142, 143
  Sumida Hokusai Museum 139, 140
  Tachibana Museum, Yanagawa 19
  Taiho Koki Sumo Museum, Hokkaido 183
  Takayama Festival Floats Exhibition Hall 142, 143
  Takayama Jinya 143
  Teshima Art Museum 39, 40
  Tokyo Metropolitan Edo-Tokyo Museum 119, 139
  Tokyo National Museum 123
  Tombo Okoku Dragonfly Kingdom, Shimanto 87
  Tonkururen Togakushi Soba Museum, Nagano 147, 148
  Trick Art Museum, Takao 119
  Tsuboya Pottery Museum, Naha 63
  Tsuruoka Art Forum 151
  Volcano Museum, Mount Aso 71
  Wakkanai Science Museum 171
  Wax Museum, Uchiko 83
  Wetland Museum, Niigata 151
  World Bags & Luggage Museum, Tokyo 118, 119
  Yamagata Museum of Art 159

N

NAGANO 146, 147, 151
  Daizen Soba Restaurant 146, 147
  Kagami-Ike Pond 148
  Okusha Shrine 147, 148
  Togakushi Forest Botanical Garden 147
  Togakushi Shrine 147
  Tonkururen Togakushi Soba Museum 147, 148
  Zenkoji Temple 147
  Zuiji-mon Gate 148

NAGASAKI 47
  Glover Garden 47
  Ground Zero 47
  Gunkanjima 47
  Gunkanjima Digital Museum 47
  Hypocentre 47
  Nagasaki Peace Museum 47
  Nagaski Penguin Aquarium 47
  Peace Park 46

NAGOYA 31, 34, 35, 36, 175
  JR Railway Museum 34, 35
  Nagoya Chunichi Dragons 127
  Nagoya City Science Museum 34, 35

NAHA 50, 51, 54, 55, 56, 63
  Former Japanese Navy Underground Headquarters 54, 55
    Tunnels 55
  Giant Tug-o'-War Rope 55, 56
  Ikutouen Pottery Studio 63
  Makishi Public Market 55
  Manko Wetlands Centre 55
  Shurijo Castle 55
  Tsuboya Pottery Museum 63

NAKASENDO WAY 7, 95, 107, 115, 119 See also Shrines & Temples
  Ena 115
  English Club 114
  Hikone 115
    Hikone Castle 114
  Hiroshige 115
  Hosokute Post-Town 115
  Ishidatami Rock Paving 115
  Jizo Pass 115
  Kaida Kogen (Plateau) 115
  Karuizawa Post-Town 115
  Kii Katsura 31
  Kiso-Fukushima 115
  Koguchi 31
  Koyasan 31
  Magome Pass 115
  Magome Post-Town 115
  Mitake Post-Town 115
  Mount Ontake 115
  Nagiso 115
  Nakatsugawa 115
  Narai Post-Town 115
  Nihonbashi Bridge 115
  Ochiai Post-Town 115

Okute Post-Town 115
Sekigahara 114, 115
Shinchaya 115
Torii Toge Pass 116
Tsumago Post-Town 115
Usui Toge Pass 115
Yokokawa 115

NAOSHIMA 39, 40
Benesse House 39, 40
Benesse House Museum of Art 39
Chichu Museum 39
Chido Museum 151
Lee Ufan Museum 39
Yayoi Kusama Pumpkin 40

NARA 110, 111, 131
Isuien Garden 110, 111
Kasuga Taisha Shrine 110, 111
Kofukuji Natural Temple 111
Kofukuji Natural Treasure Hall 111
Monsieur Pepe Restaurant 111
Okumura Museum 111
Todaiji Temple 111
Wakakusayama Hill, Nara 111
Yoshikien Garden 111

NARUTO 95
Naruto Whirlpools 95, 96
Onaruto Bridge 95, 96

National Parks
Akan Mashu National Park, Hokkaido 183
Ashizuri-Uwakai National Park, Shikoku 87
Daisetsuzan National Park, Hokkaido 167
Kushiro-Shitsugen National Park, Hokkaido 183
Rishiri Rebun Sarobetsu National Park, Hokkaido 171
Takino Suzuran Hillside National Park, Sapporo, Hokkaido 195, 196, 199
Yakushima National Park 75

Nautiluses 36, 123
Paper Nautilus 67

Nemophila 127, 128

New Year's Eve 59

Nightingale Floorboards 103

Nihonga Art 130, 131

NIIGATA 151, 152
Fukushimagata Wetland 151
Hakusan Koen Park 151
Imayo Tsukasa Sake Brewery 151
Media Ship Building 151
Nakanokuchi River 151
Niigata Manga Animation Museum 150, 151
Niigata Sake Museum 151, 152
Urauchi River 63
Wetland Museum 151

NIKKO 163, 164
Kannon-do Shrine 163
Ken-do 163
Lake Yunoko 163
Nikko Botanical Garden 163
Nikko Railway Station 162, 163
Nikko Suginamiki Youth Hostel 163
Potato Cafe 163
Senjogahara Moor 162, 163
Shimotsukeoosawa 163
Toshogu Shrine 163, 164
Yumoto Onsen 163

Ningyo See FUKUOKA, Hakata dolls

NISHI-IYA 98

NIYODO 91
Niyodo River 91
Tombo-Chan 91, 92
Tosawashi Kogeimura 'Qraud' 91
Yakatabune (Houseboat) 91, 92

Noborigama (Hill Climbing Kiln) 50, 51

Notsuke Peninsula, Hokkaido 179

O

O-Bon Festival 195

Octopus 171

ODAWARA 131

OFUKUTE
Gallery Hakurin Tokachi, Nakasatsunai 186
Nakasatsunai Art Village 186

O-Henro 95

OITA 66, 67
Takasakiyama Monkey Park, Oita 67
Umitamago Aquarium 67

Okama Crater Lake 159

OKAYAMA 39, 79, 80
Koraku-en 39, 79
Naked Man Festival (Saidaiji Eyo) 79, 80
Okayama Koraku-en 38
Saidai Temple 79

OKINAWA 50, 51, 52, 54, 55, 59, 63, 67, 103
Arboretum Churaumi 52
Cape Maeda 60
Churaumi Aquarium and Ocean Park 51, 52
Mibaru Beach 59
Minatogawa Man 58
Okinawa World 58, 59
Peace Memorial Park 54, 55
Pillar of Peace 55
Sefa-Utaki 59
Tokashiki Island 59, 60
Tsuikin Laquerware Technique 51
Valley of Gangala 58, 59
Yomitan Pottery Village 50, 51

Okonomiyaki (Cabbage Pancake) 15, 167

Olympic Games 147, 191
Olympic Ski Slopes 7

Omelettes 19

OMIYA 138
Omiya Bonsai Art Museum 135
Saitama Railway Museum 138, 139

Onsens (Hot Springs) 23, 30, 31, 71, 115, 171, 203

Orcas 179

OSAKA 26, 27, 31, 111
Museum of Oriental Ceramics 26, 27
Namba 31
Nanko Wild Bird Sanctuary 27
Osaka Aquarium Kaiyukan 27
Osaka Castle 27
Umeda Station 27

OTARU 195
Sakaimachi Street 195
Temiya Line 195

OTOFUKE 187
Nakasatsunai Art Village 186, 187
Gallery Hakurin Tokachi 187
Nakasatsunai Art Village Garden 187
Toipirka Kitaobihiro Youth Hostel 187

P

Pandas 123

Paper-Making 91

Parades 123

Parasitology 123

Parking 67

Passenger Injury 135

Pelican 67

Penguins 35, 166, 167

Peonies 131

Pets 135
Dogs 135
Hedgehogs 59

Pharmacy 203

Phone Cards 203

Picasso 131, 159
Pickle Rice 71
Pickles 19
Picnics 119
Pilgrims 82, 83, 95
  Pilgrim Shop 94
Pit Vipers 187
Planning 7
Plates 51
Polar Bears 167
Police 202
Pottery 143
Princess Diana 155
Ptarmigans 146
Pteropods 175
Public Holidays 202
  Golden Week 202
Public Phones 203
Public Transport 7
Puppetry 84
Puppies 50, 51
Python 58

Q
QB House Haircuts 167
Qraud Paper-Making 91

R
Railway Stations
  Railway Station Signage 203
Ramen 15
RAUSU 179, 180
  Geyser 179
  Goko Lakes 179
  Lake Rausu 179
  Mount Rausu 178, 179
  Rusa Field House 179
  Shiretoko National Park 179
  Shiretoko Pass 178, 179
Rebun Island 171, 172
  Eidelweiss 171
  Rishiri Rebun Sarobetsu National Park 171
Recycling 202
Red-Crowned Cranes 179
Rei Naito (Artist) 39
Restaurants 202
Rhododendrons 131
Rice Cakes 159
Rice Crackers
  Rice Cracker-Making Class 139
Rickshaws 107
Rim of Fire, Mount Aso 71
Rishiri Island 171, 172
Rishiri Rebun Sarobetsu National Park, Hokkaido 171, 172
Roaming Charges 203
Robata (Barbecue Restaurant) 183
Rodin 131
Romaji 203
Romance Car Train 131

Rugosa Roses 99
Ryokans 31, 115
Ryue Nishizawa (Architect) 39
Ryukyu 59
Ryukyu Glass Village, Okinawa 50, 51

S
Safety Tips 202
SAGA 43
  Saga Hot-Air Balloon Museum 43, 44
  Saga Youth Hostel 43
SAIJO SAKE TOWN 43
SAITAMA 135, 136, 139
  Higashi-Urawa Station 135
  'Papagallo e Topo' Cockatiel Farm 135, 136
  Saitama Railway Museum 138, 139
  Saitama Seibu Lions 199
  Salon de Koala 135
Sake Breweries 42, 43, 143, 151, 155
Sakhalin Island 171
Salads 19
Salmon 179
SAMANI 187, 188
  Peridotite Plaza 187
Samurai 78, 79
  Ken-Do (Samurai Training) 163
  Samurai Residences 155
Sandankyo Gorge 43, 44
Sand Dollars 71
SAPPORO 7, 75, 166, 167, 191, 195, 199, 200
  Ainu Museum, Hokkaido University 191
  Auroratown 191
  Austrian House 199
  Clock Tower 191
  Easter Island Moai Statues 198, 199
  Former Government Building 195
  Grids Hostel & Hostel 167
  Hitsujigaoka Park 199
  Hokkaido University 191
  Hokkaido University Ainu Museum 191
  Hokkaido University Botanical Garden 191
  Makomanai Takino Cemetery 198, 199
  Maruyama Zoo 191
  Moerenuma Park 194, 195, 199
  Mount Moiwa 191
  Nijo Fish Market 195
  Odori Park 190, 191, 192
  Okurayama Olympic Ski Jump 191, 192, 199
  Okurayama Winter Sports Museum 191, 192, 195, 199
  Otaru Beer Festival 195
  Paseo 199
  Poletown 191
  Sapporo Art Museum and Craft Buildings 199, 200
  Sapporo Art Park 195, 199, 200
  Sapporo Arts Festival 191, 199
  Sapporo Dome 198, 199
  Sapporo Snow Festival Museum 199
  Snow Festival 7, 191, 199
  Susukino 166, 167, 191, 195
  Takino Suzuran Hillside National Park 195
  Tapas Bar 167
  Tonden Restaurant 191, 195, 199
  Toyohira-Ku 190
  Tozai Line 191
  Tsuruga Buffet Dining 195
  TV Tower
    TV Tower Observatory 191
Sashimi 19
Satsuma Rebellion 79
SATSUMASENDAI 79
Scallops 171, 179
Sculptures 40, 111, 130, 159

Sea Angels 174, 175
Sea Cucumbers 171, 195
Seals 166, 171
Sea of Japan 99
Sea Urchins 179
Seaweeds (Kelp, Konbu) 95, 171, 179, 180, 182, 183, 195
Seismic Isolation 111
Seniors 7
Seniors Discounts 203
Seven Eleven 127, 135
Shabu-Shabu See Hot-Pots (Nabe, Shabu-Shabu)
Shamisen (Musical Instrument) 154, 155
Shika-no-Fun (Deer Biscuits) 111
Shiki-Shima 163
SHIKOKU 8, 39, 83, 87, 95, 99, 103
   Ashizuri-Uwakai National Park 87
   Shikoku 88-Temple Pilgrimage 83, 87, 95
   Yatsushiro 79
SHIMANTO 86, 87, 91
   Tombo Okoku Dragonfly Kingdom 86, 87
Shingi 79
SHIN-HAKODATE HOKUTO 167
SHINHIDAKA (SHIZUNAI) 186, 187
   Mount Apoi Geopark 187, 188
Shinkansen 203
Shinkansens 11, 27, 34, 35, 79, 99, 139, 147, 163
   Gran Class 167
   Hayabusa 167
   Mizuho 11
   Nozomi 11
Shinto 11, 19, 60
SHIRAWAWA-GO 142, 143
Shiretoko National Park, Hokkaido 179
   Goko Lakes 179
SHIRONE 150
   Shirone Kite Festival 150
Shisa 60
SHIZUNAI (SHINHIDAKA) 187
Shrimp
   Farmed Shrimp 75
Shrines & Temples
   Aoshima Shrine 72
   Chikurinji Temple, Kochi 91
   Chinese Kantel-byo Mausoleum, Kobe 111, 112
   Fushimi-Inari Shrine, Kyoto 102, 103
   Ginkakuji Silver Temple, Kyoto 103
   Hakozakigu Shrine, Fukuoka 11
   Higashi Honganji Temple, Kyoto 107
   Honganji Kobe Betsuin Temple 111
   Hongu Taisha Shrine, Kumano-Kodo Pilgrimage 31, 32
   Hotsumisaki Temple, Cape Muroto 95
   Ise Grand Shrine (Ise Jingu) 31, 35
      Geku (Toyouke Dai-Jingu) Outer Shrine 31, 32, 35
      Naiku (Kotai Jingu) Inner Shrine 35
   Itsukushima Shrine, Miyajima 43
   Jizoji Temple, Tokushima 95
   Kanda Myojin Shrine, Tokyo 135
   Kannon 107
   Kannon-do Shrine, Nikko 163
   Kasuga Taisha Shrine, Nara 110, 111
   Kinkakuji Golden Temple, Kyoto 106, 107
   Kofukuji Natural Treasure Hall, Nara 111
   Kofukuji Temple, Nara 111
   Kongofukuji Temple, Cape Ashizuri 86, 87
   Miyajima 'Floating' Shrine 42, 43
   Nachi Taisha Shrine, Kumano-Kodo Pilgrimage 30, 31
   Nanzenji Temple, Kyoto 103, 104
   Nanzoin Temple, Fukuoka 11
   Nezu Shrine, Tokyo 123
   Nishi Honganji Temple, Kyoto 107
   Okusha Shrine, Nagano 147, 148
   Ryoanji Temple, Kyoto 107
   Saidai Temple, Okayama 79
   Sanjusangendo Temple & Hall, Kyoto 107, 108
   Sennyuji Temple, Kyoto 103
   Sensoji Temple, Tokyo 123, 124, 139, 140
   Shikoku 88-Temple Pilgrimage 87, 91, 95
      Temples 1-5, Tokushima 95
   Shingu Shrine, Kumano-Kodo Pilgrimage 31
   Sukyo Mahikari World Shrine, Takayama 143
   Taisanji Temple, Matsuyama 82, 83
   Takaosan Yakuoin Temple, Mount Takao 119
   Tenmangu Shrine, Fukuoka 23
   Todaiji Temple, Nara 111
   Tofukuji Temple, Kyoto 103
   Togakushi Shrine, Nagano 147
   Toji Temple, Kyoto 103, 107, 108
   Toshogu Shrine, Nikko 163, 164
   Ushiku Daibutsu, Tokyo 134
   Yushima Seido (Shrine of Confucius), Tokyo 135
   Zenkoji Temple, Nagano 147
Sightseeing Train 98
SIM Cards 203
Skiing 7
Skunk Cabbages 147, 148
Smoking 19
Snorkelling 59, 60, 63
Snow 99, 116, 171, 203
   Snow Fences 175
   Snow Wall (Uki-no-Otani) 146, 147
Soba Noodles 135, 147, 148
   Soba 100% Buckwheat Noodles 143
Sounkyo Gorge 7, 167
   Ryusei No Taki 7
SOUNKYO ONSEN 167
Soymilk Skin 163
Spam 63
Speed Limit 167
Sperm Whales 179
Spirits See Alcoholic Drinks
Sports 202
Star-Sand Beach 63
Stonehenge 199
Storage Lockers 24, 43, 202, 203
Strawberry Picking 128
Street Dancers 124
Street Food 91
Subtropical Plants 71
Sugar 63
Suicide 135
Suikinkutsu 82, 83, 154, 155
SUKUMO 87, 88
   Ashizuri-Uwakai National Park 87
   Hotel Avan 87
   Matsuda River 87
   Oshima Island 87, 88
Sumo 183
   Grand Sumo Tournaments 7, 139, 175
   Gyoji (Referrees) 139
   Rikishi (Wrestlers) 139
   Sumo Stadium 139
Super Hakuto Limited Express 167
Supermarkets 135, 202, 203
Sushi 11, 19
Swimming 7, 99, 195

Swimming Pools 15

T

Tadao Ando (Architect) 111, 155, 199

Taiko Drums 15, 16, 35, 59, 155

Taishokoto (Musical Instrument) 142, 143

TAKAMATSU 39
  Ritsurin Garden 38, 39

TAKAMORI 47, 48
  Ganbare Kumamoto! Manga Yosegaki Train 48
  Natural Springs 47, 48
  Takamori Tunnel Park 47
  Youth Hostel Murataya Ryokan 47

TAKAO
  Trick Art Museum 119

TAKAYAMA 139, 142, 143, 144
  Hida Beef 143
  Hida Folk Village 143
  Hida Takayama Museum of Art 143, 144
  Sanmachi Suji (Historic District) 143
  Shirakawa-go 142, 143
  Sukyo Mahikari World Shrine 143
  Takayama Festival Floats Exhibition Hall 142, 143
  Takayama Jinya 142, 143
    Torture Room 143

Takino Suzuran Hillside National Park, Sapporo 195, 196, 199

TANBO-ART 155, 156

Tapeworm 122

Tateyama Kurobe Alpine Route 147
  Kurobe 146
  Ogizawa 147
  Snow Wall (Uki-no-Otani) 146, 147
    Snow Wall Walk 146

Tattoos 203

TAZAWAKO 8, 159
  Nyuto Onsen 158, 159
  Tatsuko Statue 158
  Tazawako Heart Herb Garden 159
  That Sounds Good Jazz Pension 159

Tea Ceremony 139

Teishoku (Set Meals) 139

Tempura 19, 91

Tenugui (Ken-Do Headscarf) 163

TESHIKAGA 179, 183
  Lake Akan 183
  Lake Kussharo 183
  Lake Mashu 183
  Lake Onneto 183
  Marimo Algae Balls 183
  Onneto Hot Waterfall 183
  Wakoto Peninsula 183

TESHIMA 39
  Teshima Art Museum 39, 40

The Great Wave of Kanagawa 139

Ticks 187

Tipping 7, 95

Tofu Factory 55

Tofuyo 55

Toilets 7

Tokoro Curling Centre 174, 175

TOKUSHIMA 91, 95, 96, 99
  Awa Odori Dance Show 95, 96
  Central Park 95
  City Boat Tour 95
  Jizoji Temple 95
  Temples 1-5, Tokushima 95
  Tokushima Castle 96

TOKYO 11, 59, 107, 115, 119, 123, 127, 135, 139, 140, 163
  Akihabara 134, 135
  Antiques Market 119, 120
  Asakusa 119, 123, 139
  Big B Shoe Shop 119
  Chabara 135
  Daibutsu Great Buddha, Ushiku 134, 135
  Denboin Garden 123
  Drum Museum 119
  Electric Town 135
  Ginza 115, 119
  Go-Karts 134
  Heiwa-Dori Street 55
  Hibiya Park 123, 124
  Ikebukuro 124
    Ikebukuro Station 135
  Imperial Palace Tokyo 119, 138, 139
  International Forum Building 119, 120, 139
  Japan Folk Crafts Museum and West Hall 139
  Kabukiza Theatre 119
  Kaminarimon Gate 123
  Kanda Myojin Shrine 135
  Kappabashi Street 122, 123
  Kuramae 119, 123
  Magano 123
  Marunouchi 119
  National Art Centre 123
  National Museum of Modern Art & Crafts Annex 123, 139
  Nezu Shrine 123
  Omiya Bonsai Art Museum 135, 139
  Orange Street 119
  Owl Cafes 120
  Palace East Gardens 119, 139
  Parasitology Museum 122
  Roppongi Hills 123
  Ryogoku 119, 139
  Ryogoku Kokugikan Sumo Stadium 119, 140
  Ryogoku Kokugikan Sumo Stadium Museum 119
  Saitama Railway Museum 138, 139
  Sakura Street 115
  Sanja Festival 139, 140
  Sensoji Temple 123, 124, 139, 140
  Setagaya Tea Ceremony Studio Lempicka 138
  Shibuya 139
  Shinden 139
  Shinjuku 131
  Sumida Hokusai Museum 139, 140
  Sumida Park 118, 119
  Sumida River 119
  Sunshine Aquarium 123, 124
  Sunshine City 123
  Tokyo 2k540 Crafts District 135
  Tokyo Institute for Nature Study 122, 123
  Tokyo Metropolitan Edo-Tokyo Museum 119, 139
  Tokyo Midtown 123
  Tokyo National Museum 123
  Tokyo Skytree 119
  Tokyo Station 115, 120
  Tsukuji Fish Market 123
  Tuna Auction 123
  Ueno Park 119
  Ueno Station 163
  Ueno Zoo 123
  World Bags & Luggage Museum 118, 119
  Yanaka Cemetery 123
  Yanaka Ginza 123
  Yurakucho 119
  Yushima Seido (Shrine of Confucius) 135

Tokyu Hands 195

TOYAMA 147

Transport 202

Travel Insurance 203

Triennale 39

Trip Advisor 103

Tsunamis 51, 56, 83, 202

TSURUOKA 151, 152
  Chidokan Clan School 151
  Chido Museum 151
  Kamo Jellyfish Aquarium 151, 152
  Mount Haguro 151, 152
  Tsuruoka Art Forum 151
  Tsuruoka Cultural Centre 151, 152
  Tsuruoka Park 151

Tulips 103, 124

Typhoons 15, 83, 167, 203

U

UCHIKO 83, 84
    History & Folklore Museum, Museum of Commercial & Domestic Life 83
    Ikazaki Kite Museum 83
    Uchiko-Za Theatre 83, 84
    Wax Museum 83

V

Van Gogh 159

Vegemite 15

Vegetables 11, 14, 19
    Edamame Beans 162, 163
    Purple Sweet Potatoes (Beni-Imo) 51, 55

Vending Machines 7, 187, 203

Visas
    Six-Month Sightseeing Visas 7, 11
    Temporary Three-Month Tourist Visa 11
    Toursit Visa 203

Volcanoes 47, 79

Voltage 202

W

WAKKANAI 167, 170, 171, 175
    Breakwater Dome & Colonnade 171
    Cape Noshappu 171
    Cape Soya 171
    Horonobe Visitor Centre 171
    Mega Solar Plant 171
    Meguma Marsh 171
    Milk Road 171
    Mount Rishiri 172
    Onuma Bird House 171
    Pension Arumeria 171
    Rishiri Rebun Sarobetsu National Park 171
    Sakhalin Island 171
    Sarobetsu Visitor Centre 171
    Sarobetsu Wetland 172
    Soya Hills 171
    Stellar's Sea Eagles 171
    Tower of Prayer for Korean Airlines Flight 007 172
    Wakkanai Aquarium & Science Museum 171
    Wakkanai Station 171
    White-Tailed Eagles 171

Walking Sticks 95

Water 203

Water Droppers 27

Waterfalls 63, 75

Weather 203

Wedding 127

Whales 59, 123, 179

Whale Sharks 26, 27, 52

Wi-Fi 202

Wine See Alcoholic Drinks

Wisterias 126, 127

Woodblocks 139

Woodpeckers 168, 179

Y

YAEYAMA ISLANDS 63, 103
    Hirakubozaki Lighthouse 63
    Iriomote Island 63
    Ishigaki 63
    Kabira Beach 62, 63
    Satakentia liukiuensis (Palm) 63
    Taketomi Island 63
    Urauchi River 64
    Yonehara 63

Yakitori See Chicken

Yakkan Shoumei (Medicine Importation Form) 7

YAKUSHIMA 74, 75, 76, 79
    Hirauchi Kaichu Onsen 75
    Jomonsugi Cedar 75
    Kuchinoerabujima 75
    Kusugawa Onsen 75
    Miyanoura 75
    Oko-no-Taki Waterfall 75
    Orange House Cottage 75
    Sanpiro-no-Taki Waterfall 75
    Shiratani Unsuikyo Ravine 75, 76
    Taikoiwa Rock 75, 76
    Yakushima National Park 75
    Yakusugi 75
    Yakusugi Land 75, 76

Yakushima National Park 75

YAMAGATA 159
    Yamagata Castle 159
    Yamagata Museum of Art 159

YANAGAWA
    Tachibana Museum 19

Yayoi 15, 16
    Burial Urns 16

Yayoiken Restaurant 11, 139

Yayoi Kusama (Artist) 39, 40

YOKOHAMA 127
    Maritime Museum 111
    Meriken Park Earthquake Memorial Park and Harbor Land 111
    Tsutsugo 127
    Yokohama Bay Quarter 127
    Yokohama Baystars 127
    Yokohama Garden Necklace 126, 127
    Yokohama Stadium 126, 127

Yuba (Soymilk Skin) 163

Yujiro Ishihara (Actor/Poet) 155, 156

Yukata (Summer Kimono) 11

YUMOTO ONSEN 163

Z

ZAO ONSEN 159
    Juhyo Kogen 160
    Mount Sanpokojin 160
    Zao Onsen Big Open Air Bath Dai Roten Buro 159
    Zao Sky Cable 159, 160

Zoos & Aquaria
    Asahiyama Zoo, Asahikawa 166, 167
    Churaumi Aquarium and Ocean Park, Okinawa 51, 52
    Kamo Jellyfish Aquarium, Tsuruoka 151, 152
    Kumamoto Zoo/Botanical Gardens 47
    Maruyama Zoo, Sapporo 191
    Nagaski Penguin Aquarium 47
    Osaka Aquarium Kaiyukan 27
    Shima Marineland 35
    Sunshine Aquarium, Tokyo 123, 124
    Takasakiyama Monkey Park, Oita 67
    Toba Aquarium 35, 36
    Ueno Zoo, Tokyo 123
    Umitamago Aquarium, Oita 66, 67
    Wakkanai Aquarium & Science Museum 171

www.ingramcontent.com/pod-product-compliance
Lightning Source LLC
Chambersburg PA
CBHW061132010526
44107CB00068B/2917